11/2015

SOUL
COUR...

Rita,
Thank you for
the beautiful friendship
we share.
I love you!
Jana ♡

SOUL COURAGE

Watch what happens.

TARA-JENELLE WALSCH

RAINBOW RIDGE
BOOKS

Cover and interior design by Frame25 Productions
Cover art © grafikwork, c/o Shutterstock.com

Published by:
Rainbow Ridge Books, LLC
140 Rainbow Ridge Road
Faber, Virginia 22938
www.rainbowridgebooks.com
434-361-1723

If you are unable to order this book from your local bookseller,
you may order directly from the distributor.

Square One Publishers, Inc.
115 Herricks Road
Garden City Park, NY 11040
Phone: (516) 535-2010
Fax: (516) 535-2014
Toll-free: 877-900-BOOK

Visit the author at:
www.soulcourage.com

Library of Congress Cataloging-in-Publication
Data applied for.

ISBN 978-1-937907-39-6

10 9 8 7 6 5 4 3 2 1

Printed on acid-free recycled paper in Canada

This book is dedicated to:

My Mother,
DANEENE W. KIPP
for giving me wings.

My Father,
NEALE DONALD WALSCH
for being my hero.

My Sister,
SAMANTHA A. LANGENSTEIN
for holding my heart.

CONTENTS

Chapter 1

WHO

Who are you?

Do you know?

I mean *really* know who you are, as in who's behind the curtain, past your thoughts, underneath your skin, deep inside . . . beyond your desires and joys, and below your deepest pain. The Real You.

Not what you look like, how old you are, or how much you weigh. Not what job you have, how smart you are, or what they pay. Not your upbringing, how wise you are, or what you've learned. Not what happened to you, how brave you are, or how you've been burned.

Not even who you hope to be or your future goals and dreams. The "you" that existed *before* you even took your very first breath.

Your Soul.

Do you know who you are on a Soul level?

Have you come to know that part of you at all? How does it show up in your life? Do you feel it when it does? Do you trust it?

Have you consciously invited your Soul to live with you and to be an active part of this life with your mind and body? Do you even believe that you *have* a Soul?

Oddly enough, the question "Who are you?" is rarely asked. It's a question we would ask of ourselves, of course—yet self inquiry may not be humanity's long suit.

And this is not the only inquiry that the largest number of people seem to ignore.

Chapter 2

WHY

Why are you here?

Do you believe that you came here intentionally or by happenstance? For a particular reason, or with no agenda at all?

Both of these questions—*Who are you?* and *Why are you here?*—are central to the human experience. Yet apart from history's great philosophers, theologians, and spiritual leaders, most of humanity seems to roll through generation after generation just living, without any interest in solving these riddles—or being too busy with simple survival to be concerned with them.

People everywhere seem to be running in emotional circles, trying to figure out how to make sense of it all without *addressing* the riddles. They want to fix themselves and jump-start their lives to end the blind monotony of their existence. They tend to focus on finding a solution to the immediate problem that they think will make everything better, rather than looking at who they are as a whole and how all of their beliefs, feelings, and thoughts have led them to where they are now.

While the answers to the questions above may not seem to have much to do with *whether* we survive, they will have everything to do with *how* we survive. Through the exploration of our reason for being, we will find a deeper understanding of any current dilemma or unhappiness we are facing.

We have a choice to live as happy, joyful beings, regardless of our exterior circumstances, or move through our days closed off to the real joys of life—which will have little to *do* with our circumstances.

Life's Agenda: Bigger Than You Think

I certainly can't imagine that we are on this planet simply to eat, work, and sleep. And we aren't here just to procreate and keep humanity going, because if we were, all of us would have children. Why, then, *are* we here?

I believe it's for a much larger reason.

Some say that the human body is a vehicle for the Soul; that each one of us is a Soul that has a body, a spiritual being that has become physical, not simply a physical entity. I agree with them. And if *all* of us believed that, many of us would have to admit that we've had it backward for hundreds of years. We would have to question life at the deepest level regarding love, religion, sex, politics—all of it. We'd have to question *ourselves* at the deepest level.

Our reason for existence would be shaken up so vigorously that the coordinates of our current understanding would change entirely. We would no longer be able to get away with preoccupying ourselves with our physical appearance or the amount of money we make. We would no longer be able to self-justify inflicting pain on others. We would no longer feel that we had to hide behind masks to protect our True Selves.

If we were to truly believe that we are all Souls living through a human body, we would be deeply motivated to treat others with kindness, look them in the eyes, knowing that they were one of us. We would have to *feel*.

But the beliefs about who we are aren't collective. Neither are the beliefs about why we're here. And given millions of diverse and scattered beliefs about these matters, it's no wonder we feel separate from each other, and so often find ourselves at war.

Knowing this and seeing it throughout life, the first question of anyone exploring the idea of the Soul would be: Why would the Soul even desire to come to physicality? Why would it choose to engage in such an experience?

Like so many of us, I, too, have pondered these questions, wondering what the point of life really is and why we're all here in the world. My mind has long been serenading my Soul with the long-standing inquiry, *"What's it all about, Alfie?"*

The answer that always sings back to me is that the Soul has taken the journey to physicality so that it may experience all the daily joys and challenges, elations and anxieties, tears and laughter that are part of human life, knowing that these are its greatest opportunities to *feel* what it already *knows*.

What it knows is that its natural state is oneness with all of life. It is clear that there's no separation between it and anything else. But it cannot *feel* oneness outside the physical, because outside the physical there is only conceptualization. Only through physical *expression* is Concept turned into Experience.

This then, is its agenda. And the quickest, most effective way for the Soul to experience oneness is for us, its physical counterpart, to fully *f e e l* whatever we are confronting in any moment—joy, fear, love, sadness (any and every emotion, not only the ones we have deemed *good* or *positive*)—then to fully *e x p r e s s* those feelings (to ourselves, others, or life), and finally, to combine those two experiences in a way that allows us to authentically *c o n n e c t* with others through the feelings we have identified and expressed. This becomes a Sacred Formula. It is a process that can be articulated and activated, by which the Soul's objective may be achieved.

The first two parts of the formula (Feel, Express) place you in touch with your True Self. They fuel the last part of the formula (Connect), which introduces the *most authentic you* to others. It is this connection with other human beings that produces our largest and most impactful experience of oneness, causing us to realize that, in fact, oneness is *not* theoretical, but *actual.*

This begs the ultimate question: If our Soul is here to experience itself experiencing oneness through Feeling, Expressing, and Connecting, shouldn't we allow ourselves to do that more fully? What's holding us back?

For many, lack of courage.

Specifically, Soul Courage.

Chapter 3

COURAGE

Most people live in fear. And what most people are afraid of is exactly what the Soul wishes to experience. Namely, feelings. Most of us have a generous amount of physical courage and mental courage, but Soul Courage may be another matter.

Soul Courage is about bringing who you really are to your life—your instinctual wisdom and endless curiosity, your feelings and the expression of them, your wonder and vulnerability, your joy and pain, your fear and excitement—all that you carry inside from before you were made physical, and all that you have picked up along the way on this human journey.

Soul Courage is about daring to be and own all of yourself without shame or judgment, apology or excuses, hiding or hindering. It's about meeting your feelings with gentle grace, expressing them with absolute freedom, and connecting with total presence.

It's about bravely being all that you encompass—body, mind, and Soul. *Feeling* into the living of your life, speaking your truth, singing your song, and revealing your true nature to yourself, to others, and to life.

And here's the best part: You already have Soul Courage.

Everyone has Soul Courage because everyone is a Soul, and the Soul encompasses the essence of all of life. But to *have* courage and to *be courageous* are two different things.

Having courage is courage in hibernation, while *being courageous* is waking courage up. It is very much like having talents. All of us have them, but many of us do not use them.

Babies are born with Soul Courage. It is not even experienced by them as *courage*, because it doesn't occur to a baby not to behave naturally, expressing every feeling. It is only after years of being pressured by life not to do so that children begin cloaking their feelings (sometimes even from themselves). And then, if they wish to explore, express, and share the deepest emotions held in the mind, they have to reach back and *call forth* the courage that resides in the Soul.

For much of our younger years it seems that we all stumble along thinking that life is about how much we have, what we look like, and who is on our arm. I say, "stumble along" because most of the time we don't even realize that we are living that way. We're caught in the day-to-day patterns of unconscious living, thinking that life is about what we are doing. That is, until something happens in our life (usually it's a major loss of some kind) that cracks us wide open, and we start thinking and feeling in a different way.

It's not that we suddenly turn into walking philosophers, poets, or hippies, but simply that we are able to look at life with a new perspective, having created experiences of such pain and joy for ourselves. We finally see clearly that, trite as it may sound, there really is *"more to life than meets the eye."* There's something more going on here than just what is happening!

The Choice Being Made by All of Us

My childhood was filled with love and joy, but my actual turning point, the moment of my life's most important realization, came as the result of pain.

For you, perhaps it was also pain. Possibly the result of a heartbreaking divorce, a near-death experience, being rescued from drug or alcohol addiction, or the departure of someone you deeply love. It could have also been the result of a joyful experience, such as receiving an unexpected inheritance, meeting the love of your life, or having children.

However you come to your life's most important realization (that life was created for us to complete the Soul's agenda and not simply the agenda of the body or the mind), once embraced, you are forever changed.

And this—*this*—is what gives all of us the desire for even more connection. We (finally!) now have an unwritten and unspoken understanding of it all in our bones. Correction: *past* our bones. We now know what the Soul has always known: We are here on the earth to experience our True Selves. We have a larger agenda than "survival" or "success." We are *in alignment* with the Soul at last.

It is this clarity that blooms the courage to pro-actively reach into ourselves, and then reach out to others from that place. We intuitively under-stand that Feel-Express-Connect is the Sacred Formula. We may not articulate it in precisely that way, we may not use those exact words, but we internally "get" the process. And that explains why it is something that we instinctively *want to do*—even though half the time we've been afraid of doing it. (It wouldn't the first time we've been afraid of following our instincts.)

Every single person reading these words right now is facing the same choice. We all are making the exact same decision in this exact same moment. Actually, every single person in your town is con-templating this exact same decision in this exact same moment. In fact, to be clear, and to be pre-cise, *every . . . single . . . waking . . .* person *in the world* is facing this same decision in this same moment.

Put in more human terms, the decision is this: How much of my heart will I open in order to *fully feel* my feelings, allowing my Soul to complete its agenda?

*How much of myself and my overall energy will I
let shine through in this moment? How much of me
am I willing to share* with Me?

We may never have thought of our journey through each day in quite this way, but we're always deciding, consciously or unconsciously, how much of our(true)selves we're going to allow ourselves to experience. And likewise, how much we will hide, protect, cloak, shrink, mask, or neglect in each moment.

We're also deciding how much of what we are feeling we want to share with others.

Many of us have limited what we allow ourselves to express by what mood we're in or who we feel comfortable with—conducting ourselves according to how "appropriate" we feel it is to be authentic with this or that person, or in a particular situation.

In a sense, we're measuring out our authenticity based on how much we feel is suitable in each circumstance and proper with each person.

Even when we're completely alone we are often not willing to share ourselves *with our Selves*. We desperately seek to distract ourselves from any feeling of inner connection, using one thing or another: watching TV, browsing the Internet, texting excessively, overeating, smoking, or even overthinking. These (and more) are our Resistance Techniques—anything to engage our mind elsewhere and escape our emotions.

We so often hide under an illusional blanket of protection to keep our feelings and deepest thoughts about life and love at a safe distance. The challenge here is that this reduces our ability to do what we came here to do—which is, may I remind you, to experience our True Self.

So every one of us is facing, actually, a two-part decision every moment of every day. Not only . . .

How much of me am I willing to share with Me?

But also . . .

How much of me am I willing to share with others?

I'm not talking about just the heaviest or saddest or most challenging feelings. The sharing of those might be reserved for closest family or friends. I'm also talking about the feelings of oneness itself, which the Soul is continually inviting us to experience *with everyone.*

Ask yourself: How much face time am I willing to grace others with? Will I actually look them in the eyes and *really* see them? And will my eyes rest with theirs long enough to allow them to really see *me*? How open will my ears be to truly listen to others with compassion? How will I use my mouth to acknowledge another through the words that I speak, or with simply a warm smile?

There is no metric system for the Soul, and likewise, no measurements of big and small when it comes to courage of the Soul. Asking yourself how much of your essence you are willing to share is not an attempt to gauge your participation in life, but rather a reminder of the gift that is always available for you, through you, to give and receive.

Is any of this important? Is your sharing with others somehow a "key" to life? Do any of these questions, and their answers, really matter?

Yes.

Chapter 4

DISTRACTION

I have personally spent years grappling with all of these questions.

The struggle I was experiencing was due to my inability to hear *who I really was*, the "inside me," the place where all my true knowledge, wisdom, and feelings lived: My Soul.

Without thought, I had turned over the reigns to a different part of myself, one that didn't require so much of my attention. Like half of the world, I had distracted myself *from myself* for years on end.

The need for a distraction became an addiction, and my particular substance of choice used in satisfying this addiction happened to be food. But pick a card, any card—it could as easily have been one of the many other distractions, or Resistance Techniques, that so many people use.

My choice to use food as a distraction led to a bona fide eating disorder—which, in turn, led to severe depression. My despondency had gone off the deep end and my eating disorder was steering the ship, seven years at the helm, draining my body of nutrients, energy, and life. I couldn't understand how I had gotten to this place, but when I think back now on why it all started, things begin to make sense. I can clearly remember the time in my life when I was so confused and overwhelmed that my "inside me" (my Soul) started to take a back seat, and the new driver of my life—pain—was on zoned-out auto-pilot, a "default" position that I later noticed myself using very often.

My addiction to using and withholding food to distract myself from feeling became so habitual that it started to fill my life, more than *life* filled my life. It was easily three-quarters of the pie chart and consumed me (ironically) so much so that the real me was elbowed right out of the room.

With my Soul sent packing, I was no longer able to feel the daily joy, wonder, creativity, or even the sadness of life, let alone share it with others. I was too depressed to even feel sad, and had unknowingly trained myself to become *indifferent* through years of using my prime Resistance Technique. Things got so critical that I was admitted to the hospital.

Two months in the Eating Disorder Unit stripped me of the ability to hide behind food and redelivered me to the world in such a defenseless state that I could finally hear my innermost thoughts again. The only thing is, I had been numbed out for so long that initially I didn't know how to handle being "me" again. So when feelings came knocking at the door, I had no idea what to do with them.

My immediate response was to fend off this wave of feelings that I used to block out (some of them very raw emotions) with food, but I quickly discovered that feelings don't like to be shut down, or told to *Talk to the Hand*. In fact, that seems to get them more aggravated, like bees being swat at.

This left me with a choice: Seek continued protection behind my defenses, or come out of hiding at last and open myself to the feelings that I was being challenged to embrace.

I made the second choice, and I now realize that the actual making of this choice was the first moment in which I demonstrated Soul Courage.

Your Search for "You"

Perhaps you've had—or are now having—a similar experience of losing your way so completely that you deeply yearn to find yourself again. You may even notice yourself still being confused at times, because you know that you don't want to return to the old, "protected" you who felt so stuck and trapped, but you also know that you don't want to expend the energy on creating a new, disingenuous you, with no guarantee that it will be "good enough." Yet you long for the emergence of a "you" that feels more whole, more alive, more . . . *you*.

You know this True Version of yourself exists because you've felt its fleeting presence through the years—you're just not sure how to go about having it around more often. In fact, the experience of losing your way is the very thing that feeds the desire to *find* your way.

When we lose our way in life, we don't know what to do or how to feel. Everyone wants a sign— we're all looking for clues that there's a reason for things, that life is deliberate and not just randomly happening. We often look to someone else or to "rules" on how to do, say, and feel things in ways that we've been programmed to see as safe, appropriate, or universally approved. But the truth is that we've known the way all along—yet bravery is required for most to travel this path, because we're not sure where it's going to take us.

That's where Soul Courage comes in. It gives us the strength to find—actually, to *create*—a place of safety. And happiness within that safety.

Embracing this courage, we can apply the wonderful three-part formula spoken of earlier: Feel-Express-Connect. I uncovered that formula through trial and error on my own journey, and it worked so well for me (it actually changed my entire life) that ever since, I've wanted to share it with everyone. So what I've done here is explain those steps, forging each of them into a separate process, so that you can apply this formula immediately in your own everyday life.

To make the steps more memorable (and to me, more meaningful!), I've translated each of the three processes into my own unique "Soul language," calling them: *Soulitude, Soulrender,* and *Soulcialize.*

In the exploration of these steps, I'm going to invite you to also take a look at the common obstacles that many of us—myself included—have so often encountered as we seek to improve how we're experiencing life. You cannot remove an obstacle until you know it's there, so this examination of stumbling blocks can be enlightening and helpful.

Then, a series of Guides will be offered to greatly empower your implementation of the third, and last, step of the sacred formula—*Soulcializing*.

Finally, I have placed at the conclusion of key chapters here a Soul Mission ("should you choose to accept it"). In each case this will include specific action steps you can take right now to place into your life, in a practical, workable way, everything that the chapter above it has offered.

I have already acknowledged, and I will say again: It is the embracing of Soul Courage that can propel us fast-forward on this, our present journey, for the Soul is constantly revealing to us our destination: the "you" for which you've been yearning.

The only question now remaining is how to get there.

Sacred Formula

PART ONE

❧

SOULITUDE

Chapter 5

FEEL

Everything starts with ourselves. *Everything.* What we think, what we feel, what we say, what we do, where we go, how we live, what we eat . . . *you get the idea.* What may not have been clear before now, however, is that our relationship with ourselves, with others, and with life is a direct result of how much of our True Selves (our Soul) we are willing to experience.

Life's real magic begins when we can distinguish between experiencing feelings from the conscious or unconscious side of ourselves. It is then that we see we have the choice to either *watch* our emotional life happen or *make* it happen. The more aware we are that we actually have this choice, the more we choose to *make* it happen—by experiencing our feelings consciously.

The preliminary to *everything* is going within and *feeling* our feelings in order to take an emotional pulse on whatever is going on *right now*. This initially takes courage since, as observed earlier, most people live in fear of their feelings because they don't know where *the feeling* of their feelings will take them.

If we ignore our feelings and continue with the moment at hand, sure, we can maintain our outward "unaffected" posture, the maintaining of which gives us the illusion of being safe, but this says nothing for authenticity. And we can only bury or ignore our inner truth for so long.

Soul Courage opens us to more awareness around thoughts and feelings; a process that will never end. But it does get easier and more natural.

The Gift of a Lifetime

When I was a little girl and would get upset, my mother would say, *"If you're going to cry, go up to your room. You have twenty minutes to feel sorry for yourself, then I expect you to come out and join the world again!"* I would then stomp upstairs through accelerated tears and fetch the key to my diary from its secret hiding place *(the lock of which my sister later jimmied open with a steak knife*—but that's another story).

This is how I discovered the gift of being alone with my feelings. Like most children, when I was very young I would react to things first (usually by crying) before I even knew how I felt about them. Being sent to my room gave me time to actually *feel* my feelings, helping me to *identify* what they were, versus just reacting to the situation at hand. I could have never have done this in the company of others. My mother had given me a life treasure. She taught me the value of what I have come to call *Soulitude*.

You may notice that many adults also instantly react (some with sarcasm, anger, etc.) before really understanding the feelings that are sponsoring that reaction. On the other hand, there are those who have taken the time to be patient and present with themselves through the process of life—without having to be sent to their room. They may even have built up enough courage through the years to be with themselves without desperately attempting to escape their own company.

That's what *Soulitude* is all about—being in a safe enough space (emotionally or physically) that you can feel all that's inside and around you with such peace that you have a deeper understanding of yourself. It's about spending down time with yourself, alone in some way where you are consciously making an effort to identify your feelings not just by thinking about them, but through the *feeling* of them.

Soulitude isn't merely about creating a refuge when something bad is happening, and it should definitely not be confused with isolation. Isolation is about pulling away from everyone and from life itself. *Soulitude* is about quiet time with yourself, and can be wonderfully helpful not only in times of stress, but as a way to take care of yourself on a regular basis. This is done by relaxing the body, turning down the mind, and listening to life from the inside.

A natural time for this can often be found in the early morning or late evening hours, when the noises and busy energies of life dim to a level low enough to allow your inner voice to be heard. After connecting with yourself in this way frequently, you'll begin to crave this time and look forward to it. This is a sign that you're getting benefit from it.

We all find or experience *Soulitude* in different ways. It doesn't really matter what you're doing, because *Soulitude* isn't about *doing*, it's about *being*. It's about letting go of your mind and *feeling* into the moment with the fewest thoughts possible. For some people, this is meditation, for others it may be sitting out in the sunshine with a cup of tea in the morning, breathing slowly, and listening to the birds. Or, it could be taking a silent walk and appreciating the soothing pace of nature.

Identifying your feelings may also look like writing from your heart without stopping to think or edit, pouring your emotions onto the page. Or, perhaps you're staring at the ceiling while lying in bed—thinking of nothing, but suddenly feeling (at last!) and understanding *everything*.

Wherever or however it is that you find the emotional safety and peace that allows you to identify your feelings without thoughts interrupting—*that* is your place of *Soulitude*.

Some of you may already know where you find *Soulitude*, some of you may not even be aware on a conscious level that you have already created *Soulitude*, and others of you may have to experiment a bit to find what takes you to that place.

But everyone will find that *Soulitude* is extraordinarily beneficial.

The Challenge

Sometimes there can be a blockage that holds us back from being quiet and alone with ourselves and feeling *into* our feelings. We find ourselves backing away from really opening up to ourselves on such a Soulful level. Sure, we squeak open every now and then, and yes, once in a blue moon we even crack *wide* open, but neither experience is consistent.

The idea, then, is to find that blockage, identify it, and find a way to release it. If you look closely, you'll find more often than not, that the blockage is pain. Pain unfelt. And also, surprisingly, joy unfelt.

Believe me, I know.

Since the discovery that my "eating disorder" was really an addiction to be distracted *from feeling*, I began to look more closely at what feelings I was avoiding. That's how I came upon what I just shared with you above. It's now clear to me that *many* of us utilize highly developed and very sophisticated Resistance Techniques. Many of us are "addicted" to distraction from pain and joy.

By "pain," I mean anything that causes emotional discomfort: fear, lack, loss, grief, anger, failure, rejection, loneliness, unworthiness, sadness, anxiety, etc.

By joy, I mean anything that feels good and lifts your spirits: love, accomplishment, success, anticipation, excitement, amusement, gratification, elation, happiness.

If we take a closer look at pain, it become apparent that most of us keep our pain on lockdown, buried beneath a running stream of adrenaline fueled by one thing or another—anything to make the discomfort go away and make the moment easier.

The minute we feel emotional pain we usually flinch from the physical feeling of pain and discomfort in our heart, thinking, "Oh, this hurts!" Then we run to find an immediate distraction of some sort—need a refresher on that list? It could be fixing a drink, excessive texting, overeating, overworking, etc.—even though in our heart we know that's not the solution. What is needed is the exact opposite. We need to honor the pain by really feeling into it. Soak into it. *Soak into our pain.*

My own life challenges around medicating myself with food, or punishing myself with the lack of food, caused me to ask myself what I was doing with my pain. That's a question that I invite you to ask yourself now—but it will take Soul Courage to answer. Read the question as if it were your first time hearing it, and see where it takes you:

What do I do with my pain?

Chapter 6

FEAR

What do you use to ease your discomfort? What is your "distraction" of choice? What are your Resistance Techniques—and how often are you conscious of using them? And if you *are* aware of what you're doing, how often do you do it anyway . . . and then justify it? Then, as you continue to see what you're doing to yourself, how often do you stop and declare that *from now on* you're going to seek a healthier way to find freedom from your dis-ease?

These questions are not meant to sound like an interrogation, but rather, are asked to increase your awareness around how you may be distracting yourself from feeling pain. Likewise, since pain and joy are equally valid and powerful emotions, both intended to be felt and expressed, we can also question ourselves in the opposite way:

What do I do with my joy?

Too often, when we receive wonderful news, our immediate response is to call a friend, post it on Facebook, fix a drink, or find another distraction, *before* we even feel into the joy. We think this is *part* of feeling the joy, but it's not. What we are doing is waiting for the reaction of the other person to give us permission to gauge the level of joy that we will allow ourselves to feel, and then we adjust our expression accordingly.

This is why many times when we share something joyful with another and we don't get the reaction we expected, we feel let down and curtail our own exuberance.

The question, then, is why don't we just feel it fully first by ourselves? What's holding us back from totally feeling our joy? Surprisingly, it's the same thing that holds us back from fully feeling our pain: Fear of not knowing where getting in touch with feelings is going to take us.

When we're feeling our pain, society tells us to put on a happy face and get over it. Most of the response we get from sharing our pain, fear, or sadness is that "we're making too much of things" or "it's all in our head." Yes, people are inclined to steer clear of someone who is feeling and emitting painful emotions fully, because these are the very feelings that they, themselves, are trying to escape.

Likewise, people are also inclined to steer clear of someone who is feeling their joyful emotions fully, because these are the very feelings that they, themselves, wish *they* were experiencing fully.

These are some of the reasons why there's so much resistance around really feeling our feelings. It takes us to a place of intensity that we don't know what we, or others, are going to do with. A place where our heart opens wide.

So often we don't allow ourselves the opportunity to open up and experience the purity of emotions, waiting to be felt in this place. We've been trained to turn around the moment we feel the sting, and reach for anything that can take us out of the moment—anything that can offer us a reprieve from our thinking mind. But if we really pay attention—if we listen closely to what's going on inside us as we steadily move about, we may hear a little voice restlessly asking, *"What's next? What can take me away from being fully here in this moment?*

What can relieve me from my fear of seeing and feeling who I truly am?"

The Attraction of the Middle Ground

All emotions carry energetic vibrations (*energy in motion*). Emotions that produce discomfort or pain carry low energetic vibrations and those that produce love or joy carry high energetic vibrations. This is where the origination of commonly used phrases such as, *"That really brought me down!"* or *"That lifted my spirits!"* emerged. This is why we often say, *"I'm feeling so low."*; or, *"I feel high on life!"*

People not only distract from the depths of pain and the heights of joy, but from *any* feeling that is higher or lower than the middle ground. The preference seems to be to stay nice and even, where it's "safe." Most people think that they won't get hurt or disappointed there, and that others will view them as "grounded" because their emotions are "kept on a leash." Sadly, those among us who actually *do* feel the highs and lows in life are often characterized as eccentric, weird, manic, over-excited, over-sensitive, etc.

Whatever happened to people having the full range of their human experience? We will benefit from continuing to ask ourselves: Why are we letting fear forever hold ourselves back from feeling anything other than nice and steady? How can we presume to "find ourselves again" without feeling all of life?

Let it be said again that this present exploration is not meant to produce shame or guilt in any way. The intention, I repeat, is to *increase your awareness* around how seldom you may be allowing yourself to fully identify and feel your feelings. This increased awareness will hopefully shift an automatic reaction of closing down and protecting to a fresh response of opening up and experiencing, which, in turn, will *expand* and not *contract* your energy which, in turn, will attract new people and opportunities your way.

The next time you feel anything painful (anxiety, sadness, anger, etc.) or anything joyful (love, accomplishment, success, etc.), you can choose *not* to cover the discomfort of your pain or the excitement of your joy with one of your regular "tools," but to instead make it the moment that you stop distracting yourself, and then fully *feel your feelings.*

It's never too late to take a moment of *Soulitude* and identify your feelings more closely;

to watch—and *change*—how you deal with discomforts and excitements in life. The opportunity to make fresh choices around this is something we are all given every day. Doing so—*taking* this opportunity to feel your feelings rather than hide from them—does, for sure, take courage. Soul Courage. But can be unbelievably rewarding.

If the thought of these rewards entices you, you may wish to think about whom you want to be every morning when you wake up. Then ask the question above—*What do I do with my pain?*—once again, but this time phrasing it a new way:

What will I do with my pain?
What will I do with my joy?
And for that matter,
What will I do with all of my feelings?

The answer suggested here is that you begin creating moments of *Soulitude* in your life (definitely give yourself such moments if you are under stress of any kind) to give yourself the personal time to identify exactly what you are feeling, and *why*. And then, it can't be emphasized too much, to *feel into* your deepest feelings. This will very organically take you to Step Two in the Sacred Formula: Express.

Remember the Formula? Feel. Express. Connect.

Having identified your emotions and really felt them, it will be quite natural for you to want to *express* them—which is a very good thing to do. Yet you would only be motivated to do so if you were sure that you had nothing to *fear* by expressing what you are feeling. You would have to know you were totally safe doing this.

There are tools with which you can create that safety. But why bother, you might ask? Is placing focus on expressing our feelings really that important?

Yes.

And here's why.

As wonderful as it is to feel and identify our emotions, if we continue to feel them over and over inside of us without release, we can begin spinning in those feelings to the point where they hold us captive.

Ironically, the way to break out of this captivity is through surrender.

Your Soul Mission—
should you choose to accept it . . .

* Begin your own Soul Courage Journal. Use this when making entries relating to the Soul Missions found at the end of several chapters.

* Ask yourself the questions, "What do I do with my pain?" and "What do I do with my Joy?" this time feeling into the answers and write them down. Make sure that you are not "thinking" about the answers rather feeling them onto the page. When you are finished writing, read the questions and answers aloud to yourself and take special note of any emotions that come up around the verbal acknowledgement of them (guilt, shame, anger, pride, joy, despair), as this is your gateway to healing.

Sacred Formula

PART TWO

❦

SOULRENDER

Chapter 7

EXPRESS

It's one thing to feel your emotions, but an entirely different thing to engage your emotions through expression. We feel our feelings on the inside, and we express them out. We can express them to ourselves, or with others, or both, in sequence. Many people, however, feel ill equipped to do either—and so do neither.

We all know how tormenting it can be to hold emotions inside. Whether it's a low vibrational feeling such as loss and grief rolling through our heart and mind over and over, or a high vibrational feeling of non-stop anticipation and excitement fluttering in our stomach, the emotion was not meant to sit idle. If we don't release our feelings through *expression*, the energy of those feelings will remain trapped in our body.

As we've noted, all feeling is energy. That energy that can be sent outside of us, to expand and release, or it can swirl around inside of us, repetitively. The choice is ours.

The energy of ongoing loss and grief, if trapped in the body, often leads to depression. The energy of ongoing anticipation and excitement, if trapped in the body, can lead to distraction. Both conditions can make living an ordered, grounded, and fruitful life very difficult.

When deeply held feelings are not consciously released through full and loving expression, all of the energy of those feelings will eventually push its way out of us and, after being pent up inside for so long, may produce what is often referred to as people "blowing up," or "snapping," or even rage. If it's a more positive energy that is pent up inside, it may produce what is often referred to as people being "manic" or "giddily out of control."

On the other hand, emotional energy that has *not* been held in, but released through expression soon after it first arises (not as an uncontrolled reaction, but as a response to how you feel inside in a loving way) is another matter. That produces healthy and rewarding results.

Making Catharsis Intentional

Ever had a good cry? This can be very cathartic. I'm not talking about sniffling at a sad movie or welling up when you see a dead squirrel in the road. That's easy. I'm talking about stepping into your pain and full on crying out loud, really allowing yourself to feel the pain, the disappointment, the fear. Every one of us has done this at least once in our life. We all know exactly what it feels like to release the energy around feelings at a level where we aren't in control of it. It's as if you have given-in to yourself and fully let go. You have surrendered to the experience and feel a huge sense of relief and freedom when it's over, and it feels as if the weight of the world has been lifted from your shoulders.

An outrageous laugh can also be cathartic. Not a one-syllable staccato laugh, or even a little longer bit of chuckling when someone says something funny. That's nothing. I'm talking about the kind of belly-shaking, eye-watering laughter that wakes up your spirit.

An ear-splitting scream can be cathartic as well. Not squealing when you see a spider or shrieking when someone comes up behind you. Too easy. I'm talking about releasing any hurt that you may unconsciously carry around deep inside you. This is not the scream of the *scared*, this is the howl and the bellow and the bawl of the *injured,* released by intentionally stopping to acknowledge and express your hurt through every cell of your body.

And speaking of being scared, every one of us has had a good scare or two in our lives. When we watch a scary movie we don't hold ourselves back from feeling and expressing. We yelp and scream sporadically, often shutting our eyes. In fact, that's the very reason people watch such movies! As a third-party participant, we give ourselves permission to *feel.* The same is true of sad movies, romantic films, or comedies. The movie business is all about evoking feelings, which is more therapeutic than we might realize. We feel safe because we are unseen, expressing these emotions in the dark.

If the feeling of all of these emotions can be so cathartic when arising spontaneously, imagine how powerful it can be to experience them *intentionally*.

Intentional catharsis happens when we release, *on purpose*, the feelings we've been holding within. And yes, that does take courage. The kind of courage that arises from a place deeper than the mind.

I call this deep level of courageous surrendering . . . *Soulrendering*.

This is the accepting of life's invitation to consciously turn inward and watch our *own* movie, then let go of the tight grip we have around our emotions and surrender to both feeling *and* expressing them.

Emotions come alive through our acceptance of them. And by acknowledging your feelings through intentional expression (exactly as you sometimes do unintentionally, as described above), you are bringing them out from within and giving them life. You are birthing your feelings.

The opportunity to *Soulrender* begins as soon as we allow ourselves to notice and acknowledge that we are *running* from expressing our feelings (of any kind) or suppressing them. The process moves forward through our understanding that any struggle and anguish we may be facing around feelings is not a reflection of our personal capability to *handle* the feelings, but merely a result of the mind's resistance to actually express them.

We know that we could handle this if we *had* to; it's just that we'd rather not *have* to. Especially if it's a painful feeling. That's just too unpleasant. And we can't predict what the outcome will be.

Yet the outcome of not expressing what we are feeling can be just as unpleasant. In fact, more so.

We've all felt the freedom that's found when we think that life has given us permission (such as in a movie theater) to fully *experience* an emotion. And it may be beneficial to see that it's not the *emotion* that is giving us freedom, but *the release of it*.

The key to creating this release is to look at the emotions that arise in day-to-day life and to view them differently: as friends, not enemies; as openings, not obstacles; and gifts, nor burdens. Then our automatic reaction will not be to completely deny the feelings until we have permission to express them, but rather, to surrender to the expression of them without waiting for a "permission-giving moment"; to do so *intentionally*, and not only experience the freedom in their release, but also the personal empowerment of consciously expressing them when we *wish* to, not only when we think we *can*.

The problem is that most of us have been living for a long time in that middle ground of safe emotional expression we spoke of earlier, and we have forgotten how to create a safe place outside of that zone.

A Friendship with Ourself

Being safe to express your feelings is about more than simply being alone. Even when we are not alone (perhaps especially when we are not alone) we need to believe deep down that we are on our own team, that we have our own back. But our mind won't truly believe that unless we have the freedom to demonstrate it to ourselves. So we are confronted with a classic Catch 22: We can't feel the freedom to do so unless we feel safe, we can't feel safe unless we feel the freedom to do so.

The solution: We can gracefully move from *Soulitude* to *Soulrender* (from feeling to expressing) by reconnecting with the bravery and innocence of the child that still lingers deep within. This is the part of us that used to sing in public or cry voraciously or scream for no reason at all ... before we were told not to.

The challenge is that when our adult self connects with that child-like part, it too often bumps into all the pain, self-slander, self-blame, and make-wrong that lingers inside the "grown up" mind. Our opportunity then is to demonstrate that we're on our own team by gently quieting the voice of our inner judge and intentionally shifting its tone to be more compassionate, accepting, and respectful of our pure, unadulterated self.

Essentially, this is us, looking out for our own best interest. The more we do this, the more we develop a friendship with ourselves. *And that friendship is what gives us a sense of safety.*

Now we've created a circle: Having re-established a caring and compassionate sense of safety inside, we naturally surrender to expressing our feelings, which gives us a sense of instant freedom, which in turn gives us a sense of our real self, which naturally leads to giving ourselves permission to love and respect ourselves (and others!) more.

It's because you probably haven't looked at your feelings this closely this consistently in a long time (if ever) that you found yourself fearing your feelings in the first place. This is natural. It's only when you come to a complete and utter stop in the process of feeling and expressing your emotions that this fear becomes detrimental.

Fear is not a bad thing. Lack of *safety* may be a bad thing, but fear and lack of safety are not the same.

Since we were children, so many of us have learned to relate to fear as if it were a hot stovetop (and that *does* represent lack of safety). As we grew older, we learned to instinctively move away before even feeling the heat. It's as though fear has become an emotional hot stovetop in our mind, and our survival instincts tell us to put fear into a "move away" zone. Yet our best interests may very well be served by moving *toward* fear.

Fear of "feeling our feelings" is our body's way of telling us that there is more going on inside our heart that is waiting to be felt and explored. When we reprogram ourselves to have a "move toward" rather than a "move away" reaction to our fear of feelings, we'll give ourselves both a reprieve from anxiety and a sense of freedom from our inner jail.

This point is being made over and over in different ways for a reason. I want to make it clear that stuffing feelings inside is not the way to a feeling of emotional safety. On the contrary, it keeps your feelings incomplete and unresolved, and if they are left unattended for very long, they can make you *un*safe—leading to behaviors that you often regret. All of this can occur if your feelings have been abandoned. You will, in fact, have abandoned yourself.

Your Soul Mission—
should you choose to accept it . . .

* Watch a sad, scary, or funny movie and give yourself permission to really cry, squeal, or laugh out loud. Pay special attention to how easily you allow yourself to express these emotions. Do they come freely and openly? Are you tentative with your release? Is it a conscious push to let them out? Make a note of this in your Soul Courage Journal.

Chapter 8

MIND

Self-abandonment arises because your mind is trying to protect you from what it "thinks" is going to happen if you feel any emotion deeply—even if you are alone when you do it.

The first thing that your mind may say will happen is that you'll reject your own feelings, telling yourself, if it's pain you're holding, that you "shouldn't feel that way." Then the mind will warn that if you decide you *should* feel that way, you may have to deal later with deep remorse, disgust, and shame around being the kind of person who feels *that way*.

If it's intense joy that you're feeling, the mind will actually convince you that if you get too excited about something, you *might make it go away*. Or, that you'll come crashing down if it does go away for any reason, and that it's better to maintain your equilibrium.

It's easy to avoid all this inner wrestling, the mind says. Simply *ignore* your feelings rather than feel them fully.

If you should be tempted to feel any emotion deeply in the presence of *others*, the mind will *really* go into high gear. It will tell you *not to do that* if you have even the slightest desire for approval and connection. It will convince you that fully feeling and expressing your emotions with others will scare people away or turn them off, producing instant disapproval and disconnection.

The mind will urgently encourage you to abandon yourself and your feelings as a "preemptive strike," spelling out for you that it's better to abandon *yourself first* before anyone else abandons *you*. *"At least this way it won't hurt so bad,"* your mind reasons.

Your opportunity is to re-mind yourself that this fear *is*, in fact, a signal that you're feeling pretty strongly about something, and that the best way to deal with any strong emotion is to release it by *expressing it*.

The Feeling Decoder

Until now we've been paying a lot of attention to the role of the mind and the desire of the Soul. Yet as discussed at the outset of this exploration, we are three-part beings, made up of body, mind, and Soul. So it's important to note that the body plays a large part in the *Soulrendering* process as well.

The body is a feeling *decoder*. We are, then, going to want to pay as much attention to it as we do to our mind. When encountering any deep emotion, how does your stomach feel? Queasy? Tied in a knot? Filled with butterflies? Are there any physical aches or cramps anywhere else in your body? How does your heart feel? Heartsick and heavy, or light and joyful?

By making this quick assessment of your present physical experience, you are, literally, feeling *what your feelings feel like*. Knowing this allows us to acknowledge and breathe into the feeling more fully, because you're paying attention to the physical side of it, rather than trying to ignore that, or operate on top of it and overcome it.

Feeling into your feelings is about being with what you're feeling *on every level*. Not just mentally, or spiritually, but physically as well. When

Soulrendering, you drop your defenses at all levels—spiritually ("Advanced Souls do not feel this way"), mentally ("Don't go there!"), and physically ("I think I'll have a drink." "I really should do those dishes." "Now where did I put that cellphone?").

When we resist our Resistance Techniques, we free ourselves at all of those levels. It's understood, of course, that we usually can't allow ourselves the same degree of expression in public as we might in private, but that doesn't mean we have to shut down our feelings altogether. We can still bring attention to our bodily sensations, feel the emotions that have created them, and express those feelings in a way that is comfortable and in harmony with our present environment.

Most of us "self-edit" this way already. The trick is to not edit the self out of a strong feeling entirely, putting it on hold until later—and then allow "later" to never come. This repression or suppression of emotions does not and cannot lead to vibrant mental and physical health.

The Full Enchilada

We can now see that when you "surrender to *Soulrendering,*" it creates a deep connection with the most real and genuine part of you that you've kept hidden behind all the bodily protection and mind chatter—the connection with yourself for which you have longed. You are reuniting with the tender part of yourself that feels so similar to who you were as a child: your Soul.

Letting go may sound easy in relation to stopping all of those things that you discovered you've been using to mask your feelings, but *Soulrendering* is one of the most advanced practices for spiritual growth. Perhaps you're even doing the work on yourself already (going to retreats, reading self-help books, etc.), but none of those things can hold a candle to listening to your own inner guidance and surrendering to the deepest part of you.

I remember how it felt hearing my inner voice request that I *Soulrender* after I had just done all that work rehabilitating in the hospital. The mere suggestion jolted me right back into the physical and mental fear that plagued me during all the earlier years of my life, and that created all the bodily protections and mental distractions that led to my eating disorder to begin with.

But my experience in the hospital allowed me to see and finally understand that circumstances only become hard and treacherous when we're fighting against them at every level all the time. It was through my hospitalization that the ultimate life question and biggest case for *Soulrendering* surfaced:

Why do we struggle, using only two-thirds of what we've got (our mind and our body), when we have the full enchilada (body, mind, and Soul) at our disposal to totally free ourselves?

I've shared with you the answer that I found: Fear. And I've offered a solution: Make fear your friend, opening you to what you've been avoiding, and releasing you from that avoidance to take you to a place of freedom and emotional peace. Finally, I've reminded you of the antidote that's always available to you: Soul Courage.

Of course, you have to believe that you *are* a Soul first, for any of this to make sense. You have to believe that you *are* a three-part, not merely a two-part, being.

When you remember that it is your birthright to feel, that it is your *nature* to feel, that it is your Soul's *desire* to feel—the more comfortable you become with delving into life's highs and lows fully and naturally. Then, as you do this consistently, you'll begin to welcome the process of *Soulrendering* and return to it frequently as a pathway to your innermost guidance.

The more you consciously *Soulrender* to the expression of your feelings, the more you'll witness firsthand the drastic difference in how life responds to living from a place of emotional openness and geniality versus a place of resistance, hiding, and fear. Everything will feel as if it's a big mirror, showing you who you are from a new surrendering angle versus who you once were from a resistance angle.

The act of *committing* to drop your protective walls will immediately heighten your awareness of the Resistance Techniques that you use to distract yourself from feeling. You will notice that your resistance was running on autopilot for years, and that even though it wasn't working for you, you were so used to living with it that most of the time you didn't even realize how much discomfort it was causing you. This is similar to getting glasses for the first time and suddenly being able to see clearly, giving you the "eye-opening" realization that you had been living unfocused for so long.

You'll also raise your awareness around how often and how fully you now actually do allow yourself to feel and express those feelings. You will see that this has created an inner shift toward greater peace and emotional balance, a shift so obvious to you that you'll *consciously* begin enrolling and employing *all* the aspects of who you are, teaming them up for your highest good.

You'll suddenly understand that you *are* your Soul, *manifested*, and that there's no separation between the three parts of you. And as you step into this open space that awaits within, you'll begin to feel a love for yourself so deeply that it rolls into a new love for others. This may very well be one of the biggest secrets of all time; a gateway to joy that so few seem to know about.

At last, your life will feel good. At last, it will make sense.

Unless you allow yourself to be deceived by your Default.

Your Soul Mission—
should you choose to accept it . . .

✳ Hold a special awareness around your emotions for the rest of the day, taking notice of when you consciously feel your feelings, and choose to deliberately *Soulrender* to the expression of them in some way (either verbally or physically).

✳ Journal your findings later that evening and share with yourself any feelings that may have come up as a result of *Soulrendering* into expression.

Chapter 9

DEFAULT

Living your life by default is not living your life. You're *repeating* your life, over and over.

Each of us has a Default Mechanism, a subconscious pattern of returning to memories of previous experiences in your mind to find a response to a *current* experience. Even if you're no longer using your tried and true Resistance Techniques to divert you from feeling your feelings, you may still find yourself blocked from your true emotions by your Default.

The two are not the same. Your Resistance Technique is your "distraction of choice" (incessant texting or tweeting, overeating, drinking, smoking, overworking, etc.), which is an *action,* while your Default is your "energy of choice," which produces a *thought.*

Your Default is your "Go To" energy. It powers your very first, almost automatic, reaction in response to the events of your life.

There are two energies from which we all choose: Contraction or Expansion. The energy of Contraction produces thoughts that generate feelings of concern, caution, worry, anxiety, apprehension, nervousness, tension, etc. The energy of Expansion produces thoughts that generate feelings of confidence, excitement, joy, eager anticipation, exuberance, etc.

Most of us move primarily into Contraction as our Default response to moments arising. We do this because we are being cautious, as we naturally want to protect ourselves from pain. So we usually are on guard around unexpected events.

There are also those for whom a first response to incoming events is Expansion. This is their Default. But these people are definitely in the minority.

Neither of these Defaults is "good" or "bad," they simply are what they are, and both provide instances when one would serve us better than the other. And there are occasions when all of us spontaneously combine the two, if we recognize quickly enough that our automatic first choice does not serve us. It's not often that we respond with this combination, however, because unexpected events are seen by the mind as "emergencies" of a sort, and so our Default is the First Responder.

Initially it may be difficult to distinguish between *Soulrendering* and giving in to your Default. Many of us click instantly to our Default when the opportunity to really *Soulrender* comes up. If you are sidestepping *Soulrendering* in this way, it will *seem* as if you're moving into the expression of your feelings, but you will actually be borrowing a well-used *automatic reaction* that has been filed away in your mind and body.

What has created your Default is the accumulated energy produced by your prior experience. It's how you feel *without thinking* when something occurs in your life. You don't *have* to do any fresh thinking now because you've already done your thinking about what's in the moment confronting you, *based on your past.* Your old thoughts are triggered by a familiar energy pattern that magnetizes you to them, and this powerfully diverts you from any new ideas you may have been tempted to entertain about the current moment.

It takes strength to pull away from that magnetic attraction. It takes Soul Courage.

Default Vault

You may not think that you have a Default, and that you come to each new moment in your life with original energy, but observation has shown that this is true among only a rare few. Most of us have a Default, and it is not our intellect. It's not emotion, not wisdom, pain, or joy. It's a pinch of all of those things at the same time, melded together like layers of paint on the walls in our mind—each layer representing different times in our life where we had experiences that produced an end result that was then imprinted as an intellectual concept, an emotion, our life's wisdom, our life's pain, and our life's joy.

It might help to think of your Default in just this way—as a container (you could call it your "Default vault"). Imagine it as a space in your mind where you hold all your valuables—the thoughts, understandings, and deepest feelings you've gathered from your past—and where you go especially when you're threatened or fearful about feeling and expressing an emotion in any particular moment.

Each of the thoughts produced by our Default is unique, because the energy that produces them is created from the feelings that our personal experiences have generated. Those experiences have left us feeling different levels of one thing or another: joy, pain, bliss, peace, shame, fear, excitement, and so on. The feelings that are in the majority (the "paint" that is the thickest) color our Default container.

Below are small examples to help you identify your Default. Read each question and pull insight from the answer with which you most naturally relate:

The phone rings at an odd hour and you look down to see that it's your boss.

Your first *thought* is:

1. Oh, no, what have I done wrong?

2. Oh, goodness, is she okay?

3. Wow, maybe I'll be commended for all my hard work!

4. Geez, what does she want now!

Your first *feeling* is:

1. Apprehension, concern, inner tightening

2. Excitement, warmth, curiosity

3. Mellowness, easy joy, peace

4. Mild annoyance, numbness, indifference

To demonstrate that it's not entirely about self-esteem, let's take this same example and substitute your boss with your Aunt Millie. So, as you notice her name on the phone . . .

Your first *thought* is:

1. Oh, no, who died?

2. Wow, it's Aunt Millie! How wonderful it will be to catch up!

3. Hmmm . . . I wonder who's getting married.

4. Now what does she want?

Your first *feeling* is:

1. Apprehension, concern, inner tightening

2. Excitement, warmth, curiosity

3. Mellowness, easy joy, peace

4. Mild annoyance, numbness, indifference

Try to not take this little exercise too seri-ously. And definitely resist any temptation to criticize it, saying that your own answer was not listed, or the situation was not realistic, etc. It's just a mental game to see which response you most relate to, so that you can better identify how often your thoughts and feelings are running on auto-matic, versus being organically experienced and expressed.

This might seem a little bizarre at first, but the exploration of it all can really be quite fascinating. Close your eyes and think past the rest of your mind, trying to *feel into* the thoughts and feelings that live in your Default.

What does it feel like in there?

Is the energy one of Contraction or Expansion—or a combination of both? After you identify the essence of your Default, assess whether it's working for or against your highest good most of the time.

A Default is by no means a fail-safe reliable indicator of a person's response to any given situation, but it *is* the first place that a person will go to more often than not.

Reprogramming Your Default

Thinking about the energy behind your thoughts this deeply on a day-to-day basis may seem tiresome, but it's important to do initially in order to bring awareness to how you may have been inadvertently allowing this energy to navigate you through your days and ultimately affect the course of your life.

The good news is that your Default can be adjusted so that it can work for and with you more often.

The first step in reprogramming your Default is to not be ashamed or afraid of it. Go ahead and get to know it a bit, like you did in the exercise above, and become more familiar with the energy it holds.

We can do this by allowing ourselves to really feel into a moment when we remember that our Default is on. As noted earlier, most Default responses are contracting, not expanding. So fear, doubt, and worry are very often the emotions that we frequently find ourselves covering up during the course of our days.

Yet even a consistently expansive Default is not always in our best interest. Ideally, a combination of both our expanding and contracting energies will open our vault. We need this balance of concern and caution with joy and confidence to release us from being so stuck in our old ways that we find it near impossible to experience a new moment in pure form. Fortunately, most of us know that combination and we can unlock ourselves from what we thought was going to be our safe space.

You know this pattern well, and recognize it, I'm sure, now that it's being spoken of. You'll be trucking along great during the day, and then something happens out of the blue that wakes up worry or a sense of eager anticipation. Either way, it can keep you up all night. Then you step away from your usual first response so that you can get back to living your life.

So the key to identifying, feeling, and expressing your true feelings in the moment is to be ultra aware of your Default, especially if you notice that your Default thought doesn't support you in that moment. This awareness alone will assist in stopping the old patterns from repeating themselves, and present you with an opportunity to respond to life through organic feeling. This is the place of pure creativity—when automatic responses are shelved, the blackboard is erased, and a new story about this moment can be written.

Getting to "New"

Getting out of your Default requires you to look at your Default very closely so that you know immediately when your mind has taken you there. Initially you may not be comfortable looking at your Default, but here's the thing; the more aware of it you are, the more you can recognize it—and then decide if it serves or does not serve your best interest in any given moment.

As soon as you sense that you've gone to your Default energetic response, pause for a few seconds and ask yourself silently: *"Is this really how I feel or am I carrying emotions from past experiences into this moment?"* You will immediately know the answer.

If you are sufficiently aware and honest with yourself to see that you are running on a Default response, take control right then and there. Pause and consciously breathe into what is happening in that particular moment, making sure that you give yourself the freedom to *Soulrender* to feeling and expressing whatever is coming up for you.

Do you see what you're doing? You're catching your Default in the act of trying to *pre*-form your reaction to a new experience in life so that it doesn't use recycled feelings and thoughts from an old experience. Immediately following this "bust," you're re-focusing and re-directing yourself inside to connect with how you really feel *when your Default is defeated.* You're being *creative* instead of *reactive.*

And you are being creative from the most authentic part of you, not the least. You are responding from the deepest part of you, not from your automated surface reaction. You are living from the inside out, *making life happen* from a place that is truly in alignment with your Soul.

This will change your life.

It certainly changed mine.

Your Soul Mission—
should you choose to accept it . . .

* As you become familiar with some of your Defaults, start begin to make a conscious effort to catch your Defaults "in the act" and by witnessing your old automated reaction, then consciously replacing it with a new response that carries energy, which supports your highest good. The more you do this, the faster your mind will learn to replace the old reaction with what is true for you now. Using your current response to replace your Default is a key factor in Soulrendering to your authentic feelings.

Chapter 10

THEORY

When I first realized how I had been numbing my emotions using Resistance Techniques or my Default as a means of emotional survival, and how free I could finally be by simply feeling and expressing my emotions, it felt like I had found the golden egg—as if I saw something that nobody else could see.

After my stay in the hospital (where my "distraction of choice" had been removed as an option for me), I noticed that I became more alive whenever I felt my feelings and expressed them with others. It wasn't merely the expression of *joyful* emotions that sparked a new aliveness in me; expressing contracting energy, as well, such as sadness and anxiety, did the same. What made me feel alive was *the physical act of expression itself* around any emotion. It was the *release* of emotion, not the *type* of emotion, which brought me back to life.

And there was a second thing I noticed. I saw that when I came alive, those with whom I was sharing my feelings also came alive. The authentic expression of my feelings gave them *permission* to authentically express theirs.

Suddenly it became clear to me that most people were living inside of themselves. By feeling and expressing our emotions we were "coming out," creating a spontaneous connection through an energetic exchange that enlivened each person. And what it was that made us *feel* more alive was the sudden and exciting awareness that we are one.

It almost didn't matter if expressing our feelings revealed that we agreed or disagreed. What we experienced was that we both *had* feelings we had been keeping in, and we were both expressing them in a moment of mutual courage. This exchange of deep inner feelings with another almost always made me feel closer to them. In a sense, *one* with them. And I could *feel* the oneness. I could hear myself thinking . . .

"My gosh, they have feelings just like me. They have fears and angers and joys and sorrows and ups and downs just like me. I am *not* alone. I am not all by myself in this world."

I felt so *free*. I was released from the imprisonment of my imagined emotional isolation. "We *are* all one," I remember saying to myself with the astonishment of something newly discovered. And feeling, expressing, and connecting with others *proved* it to me.

I had found the formula.

I was inspired to share this "secret" in the hope that it could open the hearts and minds of others, and totally shift their life experience. But being this excited about my new discovery quickly led to suspicion in my mind—*which had already gone to its Default*. My thoughts demanded that I test out this so-called "theory."

What if I was simply *imagining* that this new magical freedom in my heart was connected with fully feeling and then expressing my emotions? Especially since I was coming out of deep depression, maybe it was just the contrast of my current well being that was deluding me.

"Oh gosh," I thought. *"This must be tested for accuracy!"*

And that's exactly what I did.

One Saturday morning as I drove over to my Mom's house, I decided to try out my "theory" with her. So I set the intention to connect with her in this newly discovered way: through emotional availability and presence. I was curious to see if she would even notice or be affected positively by this new opening between us.

As we sat at the kitchen table drinking coffee, I *intentionally connected with her* by being totally "present" and expressing my feelings authentically. I told her how nice it was to see her, and that I was glad we were having the chance to spend some time together.

Then, nothing fancy, I simply paused for a moment, looked into her eyes, and—from the most sincere place in my heart—asked her how she was doing. I saw an energetic shift in her. I could tell that it wasn't what I was asking that affected her, but the *way* I was asking. She proceeded to share her thoughts and fears around the current happenings in her life . . . and I just listened.

Almost immediately, I found myself deeply touched by the openness of her sharing. Emotions began arising within me. This time I didn't get up for another cup of coffee, I didn't think about what

I was going to eat for dinner, I didn't pick the lint off of her sweater or smooth the table cloth that didn't need smoothing. I refused to be distracted or use any of my Resistance Techniques. I just sat with her in full presence, allowing myself to be vulnerable and really *feel* into the experience she was sharing, all the while staying available to what I was feeling about what *she* was feeling—so much so that I found myself there *with* her, instead of being in my mind, devising ways to fix her.

When she was finished talking, the most authentic and insightful response emerged from me. And then I shared my own feelings with her. I told her that I could understand how she could feel the way she was feeling about her life. I also told her how much I loved her, how beautiful she was, and how blessed I was to have her in my life.

She threw her arms around me, tears welling in her eyes, and thanked me *so* much for being there with her, telling me what a gift that experience was to her, and how safe and special she felt.

I almost couldn't believe how effusive she was about my simply being present and connecting from a genuine place. I had made a different kind of connection with my own mother.

As I drove home that afternoon, I thought to myself, *"My goodness, you're really onto something here, kid!"*

But it was only seconds later that my mind kicked in with more skepticism. *"Wait a minute . . . she is your mother after all. She would love anything you did!"*

"Hmmm, you're right," I replied out loud, as if skepticism were a person. *"I'd better continue to test this theory with more legitimate subjects."*

Road Test

A few days later I was visiting with one of my friends and I made sure to intentionally and genuinely connect from the safe and open place of (dare I say it?) my Soul. My friend shared her excitements and woes with me . . . and I just listened. I didn't divert my eyes all over the room, start petting her cat, or daydream about what I was going to do later. I was simply there with her in full presence and full feeling.

And, just as with my mother, I allowed myself to be vulnerable and really feel into the experience she was sharing in such a way that I found myself there *with* her, instead of in my mind, devising ways to fix her.

When she was finished talking, I shared my own feelings about what she had said and somehow the most authentic and insightful response emerged from me—*again!* Then I then topped it off by expressing gratitude for who she was in my life, and . . .

. . . the same thing. She cried and thanked me, telling me how special I was, and that there was no one else like me.

My ego wanted to have a field day with this, of course, but I knew at a deeper level that this wasn't about me. This was about *us*. This was about the connection we had made between our two Souls. It was, also, however, more confirmation of my growing awareness that humanity lacked, and *so craved*, deeper and more authentic connections. This was not exactly the revelation of the century—but what *was* a surprise to me was the discovery *that I could be a source of such connections.*

Now I was really rubbing my hands together with exhilarated anticipation, anxious to test this discovery in the "real world"—not just in the safety of my family and friends (whom I knew already loved me), but with complete strangers. I was bubbling with curiosity to see how far I could take this, and imagined how the world might change if people everywhere showed up like this every day.

"Hold it right there!" My skepticism snapped sternly, as if it had caught me shoplifting.

"This is a little more challenging! You can't just walk up to a complete stranger and say, Gosh, you're beautiful! *You can't approach someone you don't know (or even someone you do) and for no reason at all say,* You're amazing!

You can't just . . ."

. . . or can I?

If I really felt that way, could I share it?

I could and I did. And I soon began to consciously and intentionally make new and authentic connections daily. Once, while running errands, I decided to exercise this new practice on a "cold call" basis. I pulled up to a department store, parked the car, and sat there for a moment, preparing myself.

I didn't hum *"Ommm"* from the lowest place in my throat, or even say a prayer; I just took a few long, deep breaths and consciously dropped the walls of protection around me. First, by simply being aware of them, and then by mentally asking them to leave, replacing them with the intention to connect with the most authentic part of life, others and myself. Then I went inside.

Walking around, I carried myself differently, holding my head up and my back straight. I was generous with my face time and my personal energy, and smiled wide at people instead of turning away, even striking up *sincere* small talk when they were close by.

"Isn't this an awesome sale!" "Hey, that's a great color on you." "Wow, where did you find those?"

As I reached the checkout counter, I made sure to immediately acknowledge the lady at the register with eye contact and a warm smile.

"Hi there," I said. *"How's your day going, Stephanie?"* I spontaneously added, after quickly glancing down at her nametag.

— SCENE FREEZE —
*(A behind the scenes look
at what's really going on.)*

Okay, I hear you. That in itself isn't completely uncommon. Still, it's a step above what many semi-conscious or emotionally closed customers would do. I can say this with certainty because I've actually interviewed dozens of checkout employees and asked them about their interactions with customers throughout the day. Most customers, they said, just glance up with a quick, empty, *"How are you?"* while shuffling through their purse or wallet.

So at this point, I had already passed tryouts and made the proactive-Soul-engager team. But then I took it a step further, to give myself an inner gold star. Since my question to the sales clerk was so deliberate and personal (using people's names always gets their attention), she actually answered me.

— RE-ENTER SCENE —

"Oh, okay," she mumbled with a faint half smile.
"Just one of those days?" I asked warmly.
"It's been a really hard one, actually," she revealed, glancing up at me with watery eyes, and then continuing to check out my items.
"Oh, honey, are you alright?" I continued. I found myself genuinely caring, and she could tell.
"It's just," she paused and looked back nervously at the line, *". . . my boyfriend broke up with me last night."*

"Oh, my goodness, I'm so sorry. I know how difficult that must be," I responded, and softly touched her arm, bravely (I must say) allowing the compassion I was feeling to be physically expressed.

"Thank you," she whispered, and her eyes brightened just a bit.

This felt as good to me as it did to her. It was simple and heart opening on my part, and possibly day-altering on hers. Before I asked how she was doing, the sales clerk was alone with her feelings. I simply took a moment to *be with her* in a genuine way, opening a connection between us, and then, when she responded to that opening, I let her know that I understood how she must have been feeling. In that moment her emotional isolation ended. That small gesture lifted her spirits, I'm sure.

Through the Eyes of a Sales Clerk

If you're curious about the results of my interviews with the sales clerks, read on. They're pretty interesting. Check these statistics out:

I asked the sales clerks the following questions about the customers with whom they interacted daily and requested that they rate, on an approximate percentage scale, how much of the time they could answer "Yes."

1. Does the customer's body language convey an open, not closed, energy? *35% Yes*

2. Is the customer facing you directly (and not facing to the exit) during your interaction? *70% Yes*

3. When it is their turn, do they acknowledge you directly? *90% Yes*

4. Do they accompany verbal acknowledgment with a smile? *55% Yes*

5. Does it feel genuine? *50% Yes*

6. Do they call you by the name on your badge? *25% Yes*

7. Are they diverting their attention to other things during the transaction (their children, talking on the phone, fidgeting, etc.)? *85% Yes*

8. Do they thank you after the transaction is complete? *60% Yes*

9. Do they say goodbye and/or wish you a good day? *65% Yes*

10. Do you feel unseen by customers? *40% Yes*

11. Do you feel uplifted more often than not by your interaction with customers? *35% Yes*

12. Have you ever noticed the interaction of a customer (positive or negative) affecting your day? *95% Yes*

(End of Survey)

As I left the store I was clear that I wasn't imagining the sense of universal love and connection I felt inside, because I could see and feel that the people with whom I interacted were having the same experience. Having it mirrored by complete strangers was proof that I wasn't deluding myself or that my loved ones weren't humoring me.

No, this was for real. It was one of the amazing outcomes that resulted from me finally dropping my protective walls, peeling off laminated layers of armor, shedding my guarded skin, shucking off the barnacles.

This was a coming-out party for my Soul! This was about being vulnerable past the point of initial discomfort by sharing the *real* me with others in such a natural way that it inspired them to do the same. A domino effect with a capital "D."

More than that, this was a vibrational exchange between one Soul and another; starting with one willing heart opening into its purest essence, then extending out to another heart that was willing to receive and do the same.

I was spontaneously socializing at such an advanced level that I was intentionally connecting with myself, life, and others from a place that felt like my Soul—a place of presence, authenticity, gratitude, and good old *love of life*. A place of freedom.

I was implementing the third part of the sacred formula organically, almost by accident.

. . . I was, in fact, *Soul-cializing!*

Your Soul Mission—
should you choose to accept it . . .

* The next time you're standing in line at a store, take special notice of how the customers ahead of you interact with the clerk. Without making them wrong, notice their body language and their level of presence and personal acknowledgment to the clerk.

* You are the customer that is going to make that clerk's day. When you reach the register, make sure to be generous with your face time and personal energy, giving them full eye contact. Acknowledge them verbally and use their name. At the end of the transaction, thank them with a smile and wish them a beautiful day!

* Now, take special notice of how you feel as you walk away and leave the building. Has your energy shifted at all? Does your heart feel open? Are you smiling, either physically or emotionally inside?

Do you feel like you made a difference
in someone's day as well as your own?

Sacred Formula

PART THREE

❦

SOULCIALIZE

Chapter 11

CONNECT

Soulcialize {*Soul-shul-eyes*} *verb*
1. The act of fully and genuinely connecting with ourselves, others, and life with the mind, body, and Soul activated in unison by intentionally engaging in the full expression of our feelings.

Soulcializing is a way of being. It's the daily practice of creating truly conscious interactions by being present and being authentic. Not only being mindful of yourself and how you are feeling, but mindful of those around you and how they are feeling—and then, how you are feeling *about* how they are feeling.

It's about checking in with your personal energy, letting your walls and inner chatter drop and choosing to be fully present, then making an effort to connect by acknowledging others in some way—whether it's simply looking at them and saying hello, offering them a compliment, or striking up a conversation.

When we embrace this simple approach and integrate it into our lives, we experience ourselves as a whole being, with mind, body and Soul expressing together in harmony.

This is the kind of thing that often happens naturally when you're in a good mood, except this is different, because it doesn't happen automatically, it happens intentionally. The act of *Soulcializing* involves *consciously reminding yourself* to feel, and to share your feelings with others.

Soulcializing is *not* about being a social person; it is about being a *Soulful* person. It is about being full of your Soul, and—at last—out of your mind.

Someone may have 100,000 friends on Facebook, their phone may be constantly ringing off the hook, and they may even be going out five nights a week, lighting up the town. This person would most definitely be considered social, yet they may not actually be *Soulcializing* in the least bit.

Why? Because the act of *Socializing* is not about being out physically, it is about being "out" energetically and emotionally. It's not about having your outside go out—rather, it's about having your inside *be* out.

Soulcializing is also *not* about being unnaturally extroverted or gregarious.

This is important to know, so that you aren't misled into thinking that you're required to "be" someone you're not. *Soulcializing* isn't about changing who you are—it's the complete opposite. It's about *bringing who you are out of hiding*.

Why Soulcialize?

Since all of life is about energy, with "like" energy attracting "like" energy, and because *Soulcializing* allows everyone to experience all the energies of their whole being (body, mind, *and Soul*), you will soon begin to attract wholeness into your life. I can't think of a better reason to embrace and utilize this gentle approach to life. In doing so, I believe you'll find yourself becoming open to life in a way you may never have thought possible, and as a result, you'll be more fulfilled.

Let me give you an example: When we *Soulcialize,* we often hug others without giving it a second thought. That's our Soul instinctively reaching out and connecting with another. It wants to do this all the time.

It not only wants to reach out and connect with others, but it earnestly wants to *reach in* and connect with *you.* Your Soul wants to connect with your mind all the time. And sometimes it *does* get to reach in and connect—little scraps here and there. And if, on occasion, conditions are agreeable and things are just right, your mind will be open to your Soul connecting with it in a larger, more sustained way.

But *Soulcializing* is not about waiting for conditions to be right, or simply welcoming good things into your life. It's about intentionally *waving them in* by *creating* the right conditions.

Through all of your awareness, presence, deep feeling, and full, authentic expression, you have awakened your mind to the Soul's presence. Now it can empower your mind to manifest all of your desires—including your Soul's desire for oneness. This empowering place of unity (in place of isolation) is the perfect space from which to manifest all of life's goodness.

Everyone hopes to have abundance in his or her lives—whether it is physical abundance (better health), emotional abundance (love and connected relationships), spiritual abundance (inner clarity, purpose and wisdom), or monetary abundance (moo-la!). When we *Soulcialize*, a new flow of energy, the energy of the Soul, begins to move through and around us, and life as we know it begins to change.

We've shifted ourselves to a higher vibration, and since like energy *does* attract like energy, the mere act of focusing on the Soul by opening our heart to *more* of life (more goodness, more love, more abundance, more freedom, and more oneness) brings more of these aspects of life to us—all the result of a single decision: the choice to engage and connect with ourselves and others at a deeper level. This is about living "Soul first," which will be discussed here in just a bit. It is done through refocusing on the Soul by "checking in" with how the mind is causing you to feel at any given moment.

This is what brings the formula, Feel-Express-Connect, full circle.

The Irony of Seeking Connection

In a supreme irony, it can often be our very *desire* for connection that stops us from creating it.

We may be reluctant to use the Feel-Express-Connect formula because we know that before *connection* with others must come the *approval* of others, and we fear that by fully feeling and expressing our emotions we will scare others away or turn them off, creating a *dis*connection between us—exactly the opposite of what we desire.

This fear can lead us to the belief that it's necessary to *keep our energy aligned with other people* in order to continue staying connected. We can get so consumed with keeping the approval of others that we unconsciously match their energy in order to keep the connection. In the process, we far too often deprive ourselves of our own joy, managing the feelings of others while ignoring our own.

By going along with the behavior and energy of others despite the fact that it is not our true nature, or even the mood we're in, not only are we abandoning ourselves by not expressing our feelings, but we are also betraying ourselves by taking on someone else's behavior to gain their approval. (For instance, a really sweet boy might "energy match" the tough kids of the block in order to appear "cool.")

A more common example of this is if you're not in a mood to go out, but all of your friends are, you do it anyway, abandoning how you feel and betraying your genuine behavior in order to not be disapproved of and stay connected.

Another way that we unwittingly engage in "energy matching" with others is through lying. These are mostly "little white lies," just fibbing here and there, to preserve the current situation or relationship. Some people are aware of the lying, but just not aware of why they are doing it. They may even question themselves later, as in: *"Now why in the world did I say that to them?"* Other times people aren't even *aware* that they are fibbing. It's just something that "happens" before they know it, as a product of an unconscious survival mechanism.

Regardless of whether the fibs are something as small as agreeing with someone even though we may secretly disagree, or a more substantial lie such as fabricating an entire story about something— and despite the fact that both are spawned from the desire to maintain the flow of harmonious

energy in the moment—we are disowning ourselves in the process.

Our conscience has gotten lackadaisical and
allowed our mind to seduce us into believing that
we're protected from abandonment by sacrificing
our true selves for a moment of harmony. But it is
the opposite.

Rather than go through any part of this "energy
matching" dance, we often—when we are experiencing highs and lows in our life—unconsciously
seek out others who *we know in advance* are feeling
similar emotions about something in their life.
Then the mutual exchange, whether it is joyful or
painful, becomes a shared celebration.

This is why misery loves company. The people involved are creating a connection with their
pain, and furthering that connection through the
expressing of it, which creates an illusion of safety
and deepened compatibility between them.

This is also why when we are feeling excited
and joyful and we're around others who are feeling
the same way, our love and admiration for them is
heightened, and the like energy between us creates
an inebriation of sorts.

If there is no one around who we know is experiencing feelings similar to the ones we'd like to share, we'll retreat to those with whom we already have an existing connection, hoping that we can rely on their energy expanding or contracting in harmony with ours, according to our needs.

We often resist fully feeling and expressing around others who aren't in our safe zone or who aren't experiencing similar emotions because our mind fears that this would swing us into the danger zone. It's our thought that if we "risk" feeling and expressing ourselves fully around those whose emotional compatibility or congeniality is uncertain, our connection with them may be flawed or broken due to the raising of uncomfortable energy between us.

Our mind gives us all sorts of reasons and rationales in support of these fears. It will tell us, for instance, that if someone is not in a place of joy, it may be difficult for that person to listen to, let alone feel, another human being who is. There is also the thought that we will be disconnected through envy. What if we express our joy and it makes the other person envious and sad? That could instantly disengage us.

Likewise, our mind will convince us that if someone is not in the space of pain, it sometimes becomes unbearable to feel the pain of others. There is also the thought that we will be disconnected through another person's feeling of having little or nothing to offer us during our time of distress. That could instantly disengage us as well.

Why does our mind imagine it's likely that we'll encounter these kinds of responses from others? Once again, because many of us don't even give ourselves the gift of feeling our *own* joy and our *own* pain—so we can't imagine others being capable of feeling it *with* us.

What is unfortunate is that the very thing that we are withholding, taming, or controlling in hopes of connecting *more* with others, is the very thing that can *deepen* our connection with them.

We chase our emotional tail by denying what's deep inside, thinking it will make ourselves feel better, which makes no sense at all. That's comparable to not watering the garden to make the flowers grow. We will never shift what's on the inside until we *feel it through to the outside by expressing and connecting with it.*

So yes, it takes courage to move out of our own story and really be there with another person: Celebrating their joy in full presence without competing feelings of envy or despair around *our* lack of joy. Comforting them through their pain in full presence without competing feelings of wishing that someone would comfort us through *our* pain.

This is why the Feel-Express-Connect formula is sacred. Although it applies to everyone universally, it guides you to a place of freedom in a uniquely personal way and brings more meaning to your life than ever before. Living with Soul Courage at this level soon shows you that there is no need for courage at all, because there is truly nothing to fear.

It's like that first ride on your bike when you found your balance. It initially *seemed* like there was something to fear, but as you began to ride, you discovered there was not.

And so, it takes *Soul* Courage to find out that you don't need courage at all anymore.

Turning the Tables

Once you know that you don't have to be afraid, and that you never again have to be emotionally shut down or isolated, you'll begin to see that just as it was important to create awareness around what *you* do with *your* feelings, it can be equally beneficial to take look at what you do with the feelings of others.

Now we are talking about the full experience of *Soulcializing*. Absent this, it would be impossible to Connect. The formula would be incomplete. The promise of experiencing the joy, the fullness, and the vibrant abundance of oneness with all of life would be lost.

Soulcializing invites you to ask yourself: Do you allow others to feel their emotions when you are in their presence? Who are you *in reaction to* other people's expressed pain?

Are you so uncomfortable that you try to fix them, or shut them down in a socially acceptable way with a "there-there, it will be alright"—? Or, do you create a safe space for them to fully feel and express their pain?

Who are you in reaction to other people's expressed joy? Are you so uncomfortable that you dampen their joy with a blasé response to discount their joy, or by proposing negative concerns? Do you "throw cold water" on their exuberance?

Do you find yourself envious when others express any of their feelings freely? Perhaps even making them wrong in your mind in some way? Or, do you welcome the opportunity to "be there" for others as they move through their life's experiences?

These questions are not designed to encourage you to take responsibility for another person's feelings, but taking a look at how you *receive* the feelings of others can be a major factor in your approach to deepening your connections. This is what I was referring to earlier when I spoke of "checking in" to see how your mind is causing you to feel as you interact with others—and, for that matter, with all of life.

Unforeseen Clarity

Of course, I haven't always been this clear about all that I have just shared with you regarding this wonderful approach to life that I have called *Soulcializing*. As you know from hearing my own story, it took a major free-fall in my life and the trip to the hospital that ended it, for me to see what I had been doing to myself, and to make a new choice about who I was from that moment forward.

Thank goodness, it's not necessary for everyone to go through that kind of "awakening" experience. For some, all it takes is a sudden awareness; an unanticipated igniting of what has been lying dormant within them.

Is such a thing possible?

Absolutely. It happens all the time.

Do you remember a moment in your childhood when you suddenly had a crystal clear understanding around something, and out of the blue things began to make total sense? That's how I felt when I discovered *Soulcializing.*

To give you an idea of how I experienced this, let me share with you a moment from my childhood. It was the first time I remember having this "happy discovery" experience. I was about four years old.

I had recently gotten dressed with Mom's help and we were putting on my shoes when the phone rang and she walked out of the room temporarily. Left staring down at my untied laces, I decided to give things a try and began wrapping the crazy strings around and under, when somehow—they magically turned into a bow! The feeling inside me was one of such glee and accomplishment, pride of sudden understanding, sheer empowerment, and a deep, silly joy that made me feel more capable—— made me feel more of me.

I sat down on the bed, smiling in amazement and squealed, *"Mom! Mom! I did it! Come see!"* She darted into the room, knowing by the tone of my voice that I was okay, but that something wonderful had happened. The big reveal was appropriately staged with my knee bent up and my foot proudly positioned like a trophy on the edge of the bed.

"Wow!" she sang with approval. *"Let me see you tie the other one!"*

I paused for a minute, feeling a little unsure of myself now that I had an audience, but to my surprise, I picked up the laces and the magic worked again, as I instinctively tied a perfect bow and officially "closed" my shoe.

Although this was a small triumph, it was one that opened my mind in a new way and allowed me to *step* into myself with more assurance. This accomplishment felt more like a discovery to me at the time, an "Ah-Ha!" moment that somehow snapped me into my skin just a little bit more, allowing me to walk just a little bit taller.

This feeling of unforeseen clarity is exactly what I experienced when I suddenly realized the freedom and ease found in *Soulcializing*. Everything clicked and suddenly made sense, but on an entirely deeper level than shoe tying. Not only did the clarity around *Soulcializing* instantaneously become part of my experience, but, even more important, it expanded the mindfulness with which I entered my interactions with others, and experienced every aspect of my life.

With this increased mindfulness, I started witnessing the incredible domino effect that *Soulcializing* had on other people (my mother, my friends, strangers like store clerks), and there was no going back, there was no forgetting. The power of this gentle approach to life had touched and expanded my consciousness so deeply that it was now how I lived my life.

That's not to say that in every moment of the day I was *Soulcializing*, but the difference is that when I *wasn't*, I was very aware of it. Especially when I made *checking in* part of my regular routine.

Your Soul Mission—
should you choose to accept it . . .

* Think of a time in your experience when you *vividly remember* hiding, snuffing, and muffling your feelings in order to be approved of by someone and stay connected with them (a parent, grandparent, sibling, or close friend). Enter this in your Soul Courage Journal. Now see if there has been a time in your experience when you *vividly remember* suppressing your feelings (through overeating, drinking, or any other Resistant Technique) in order to create a *disconnection* with *yourself.* With this new awareness, the next time you notice yourself falling into this pattern, try on your Soul Courage by honoring your feelings over your inclination to energy match.

* Turn the tables for a moment and see if you can remember a time when you intentionally discouraged, or actually

stopped *others* from expressing their feelings openly around you, in order for you to stay comfortable. With this new awareness, the next time you notice yourself falling into this pattern, try on your Soul Courage by honoring *their* feelings over your desire for comfort, and support them in breaking any old patterns of energy matching.

Chapter 12

CHECK-IN

You can exponentially increase the power of the formula I've been describing here with a simple device: a series of silent questions. If you realize that you're not being fully present and *Soulcializing*, lovingly ask yourself where you are in that moment (emotionally and energetically), and who you are being in that moment. This is a quiet internal inquiry that I've referred to as a "check in."

It's not necessary to close your eyes in meditation when you ask yourself these questions. The inquiry is more of a quick clarification that surges through you. This is helpful because it holds you gently accountable to see whether you are reflecting or resisting harmony in any given situation.

There are ways to reflect harmony without the kind of "energy matching" that can take you out of your authenticity—a "trap" described earlier. Check-ins are not about pushing you to always be "on," nor to do or say something that does not reflect your truth by trying to "match" your energy to the energy outside of you. They are simply reminders to move back into presence with all that's *inside* of you, offering you an opportunity to make sure that this is what you want to feel and express.

Check-ins are not about simply avoiding being disharmonious, but also about avoiding being disingenuous. They are about being *genuinely* in harmony with life and others—and there is nothing more in harmony with life than honesty, gently expressed.

Since how you are on the inside generates what you project on the outside, taking this extra moment to silently check-in and remind yourself to be fully present and emotionally accessible gives you an understanding of how you're feeling inside *before* you *Soulcialize,* paving the way for connecting with others far more consciously, and keeping you open and accessible to life.

The more that you open up in this way, the more you will see others responding with like energy, right in front of your eyes. This phenomenon is a type of energetic transference—not at all the same as energy matching. Energy *matching* is when you consciously or unconsciously shift your energy to match that of another for their approval and connection. It's as if you are breathing their energy *in*. Energy *transference* is when the emotional energy that you are authentically feeling moves across the space to others, as if you were blowing your energy *out*.

This is why regular check-ins are important, because they bring to your attention if you are transferring or matching energy. You don't want to be sending energy into the space that you don't wish to see replicated in others.

A common example of this is when you're waiting in a long line of any sort. There is often one person who just can't contain their energy of frustration, and somehow thinks that by sharing it with others, he will legitimize his own feelings. In actuality, what happens is that he infects others through the transference of his energy.

(If you are witnessing this kind of energy transference happening in a negative way, a fun *Soulcializing* mission could be to try to shift the energy to a positive vibration. You might do this by finding what is good in the situation and bringing that up with a smile with those around you. Example: "Well, thank goodness it's a beautiful day to be standing outside. I don't often get a chance to simply enjoy the wonderful weather. My name's Tara, what's yours?" This is *Soulcializing* by lovingly connecting against energy transference.)

A broader example of energy transference can be seen in stadiums when some people become so happily enthusiastic that their energy ripples out into the mass and suddenly thousands are joining an encouraging chant to their team; or in protesting strikes where anger sometimes becomes so contagious that strikers quickly become rioters.

Energetic transference doesn't only occur when a large number of people are together. Those are merely times when it's more easily felt and seen. The transference of the energy that's alive in everyone is happening 24/7, whether we're aware of it or not.

If we could physically see energy, we would notice all sorts of it exuding from one another. In fact, there are those who can sense energy to the point where they can almost see it at times, as well as people who can "pick up on" intense emotions from others so easily that they begin to experience them as their own. We refer to these people as sensitives, empaths, intuitives, and psychics.

But it doesn't take an empath or a psychic to be able to sense energy at least at a modest level. You can feel the energy and emotions of others whenever you are fully present and intentionally bring your awareness to any situation.

We have all felt someone walk into the room who is filled with positive energy, and we often say, *"Wow, you're radiating!"* And likewise, when people are filled with negative energy, we often say (hopefully, to ourselves), *"The air is so thick you can cut it with a knife!"*

In both cases, the energy is so palpable that you become an "empath" yourself and can actually feel it, as if it has a physical presence and is floating in the air (*which it is*).

This is possible because the energy that exudes from all of us radiates in a unique energetic wave pattern—call it a "signature," if you will. We release this energy in specified intervals, or "frequencies," through our verbal and nonverbal expression.

This is important to know because it opens us to the realization that we are actually feeling the energy of other people all the time. And if we know that we are feeling the energy of *other* people, we suddenly comprehend that they can feel *our* energy in return. All of which will impel us to pay more attention to the energy that we are sending out, taking more responsibility for what we're putting into the world through our interactions.

With this new sense of energetic responsibility, we begin to see the world in an entirely new way——a more expansive way. You might even call it an enlightened way. And we begin to understand that life isn't simply about what we look like, how much money we make, our accomplishments, or children, but that it is about much, much more. We begin to understand that we are a Soul on a mission.

Living Inside-Out

Everything you do matters. The energy you carry and project affects the people around you and changes the world in a million imperceptible ways.

As with almost anything newly taken on, when we begin *Soulcializing* and feeling the freedom of living fully, we immediately become clear of the opposite and start noticing that most people live from the outside-in, waiting to see how life and others respond to them *first*, then reacting to that response. But when we *Soulcialize*, we start with how we're feeling on the inside, expressing to others from the most pure and authentic place, in doing this we're living "Soul first," from the inside-out, connecting with the truth within, then reaching out and sharing from that place with others.

We're not denying anything that's in our heart the right to be felt. Rather, we feel it fully, and once felt, move into the full expression of that feeling. And, just as important, we are not denying others the gift of *receiving* our feelings and then experiencing feelings of their own. In fact, we're *inviting* it with our approachable energy and open expression. This is where Connection lives. This is, in summary, the Soul of *Soulcializing.*

When we do this, we begin to meet others at their core level. So much so that we begin to see ourselves in and through others—and the idea of separation flies out of the window.

Yet we will find it very difficult to get to that place of oneness without an awareness of our Default (which is why particular emphasis has been placed on it in this writing) and of one other device that many of us may not be aware of using: the masking of our feelings behind a *disguise.*

Cloak Be Gone!

As mentioned earlier, all emotions, when felt in the body, create either an expanding or contacting energetic vibration. When we experience contracting emotions (fear, stress, anxiety, insecurity, overwhelm, worry, etc.) our tendency can be to close off, disengage, or isolate ourselves from others. I'm bringing this up again because there's another point I wish to make around this.

"Isolation" doesn't just refer to being alone. We can also be out and about and still isolate ourselves. This is done not by refusing to feel the emotions that we're experiencing, but by pretending we're *not* feeling what we're feeling, covering them with a facade (a "mask" or "cloak").

We learned at a very young age that the expression of certain emotions is rarely tolerated among others. Not only is the verbal expression of them seen as bothersome, even the non-verbal expression of them is unwelcome.

I've observed that many people become so uncomfortable in the presence of contracting emotions that their impulse is often to get the heck out of Dodge—and they usually do so by *leaving* us, physically or emotionally.

I also said that many of us fall into "matching energies" with others to avoid this outcome. But there's another way many often seek to escape disapproval and disconnection without getting into what for us may seem to be a distasteful or dishonest attempt to "energy match." They can simply ignore our own energy altogether by wearing what doubles as an emotional costume and shield.

From our earliest years, many of us have worn such cloaks instinctually in a continuous effort to conceal our contracting emotions that may push people away from us. We fool ourselves into believing that these cloaks keep us safe, but they don't. They simply keep us disconnected from ourselves, from others, and from life—which, essentially, produces a result exactly the opposite of what we desire, *disconnecting* us from the love of others.

Most of us can feel the difference between living from the inside out, and living from the outside-in. Aspects of our personality are either authentically expressed or they are shunned with a protective cloak to shield us in a moment of discomfort.

Another aspect of *Soulcializing* is becoming aware of when this dynamic shows up, and having the courage to break the cycle. We can do this by choosing ourselves completely, without feeling the need to energy match or cloak our True Self at any level.

When we make a conscious effort to *live Soul-first* in this way, we begin to feel more connected as a whole, allowing us to trust more and to attract more goodness into our life.

Not only are our invisible cloaks *not* protecting us, but they are shielding us from goodness. Life is flowing it to us (in the form of love, abundance, wonderful opportunities, deeper connections, new friendships, etc.), but it is bouncing right off of us as if our cloaks were bulletproof vests.

The more we start living Soul-first, the more we find that we outgrow our cloaks and they suddenly don't fit any more. They're too small! So we happily take them off . . . (*"Cloak be gone!"*) And then, there goes life, flowing its goodness as usual. Only now, our cloaks are off, so we receive.

Getting from Here to There

We've talked a lot about the strategies many of us have used to avoid expressing our truth (out of our fear of what would happen if we did so). Now let's look at some specific and empowering strategies to experience our true selves at last.

It's all very well and good to talk about *Soulcializing* as if it were something we can all embrace on a moment's notice . . . step into at the drop of a hat . . . adopt with the snap of a finger. But, in fact, most of us need a little support getting from "here" to "there."

That's where the sacred formula I discovered comes in. It offers us one map, one pathway, from our years-long hideout to the open spaces and the freedom that has been described here. This may not be the only way. I do not pretend to be the world's global expert on human psychology. But it is a way that worked for me.

At the time, I didn't know what I was doing. I mean, I wasn't using a formula that had been set out for me. I was moving forward by trial and error. I was, quite literally, "feeling" my way. Only when I looked back over my shoulder and saw the way I had come could I have articulated it for anyone else. Then the words came to me. Aha! "Feel-Express-Connect"—*that* was the formula I had stumbled upon. And ever since the moment when I realized that, when I put it all together after my hospital stay, all I've wanted to do is share it with everyone. It was just too good to keep to myself!

I knew that we already had enough closed, numb, and standoff-ish energy in the world. What we needed now was more raw, open, and vulnerable energy—more love. We needed, I believed, more of us living from our Soul. That's when I began shaping what I had newly been doing in my life—feeling, expressing, and connecting—into *ways to do that.* I labeled these: *Soulitude, Soulrender,* and *Soulcialize* to give me a starting point as I began sharing my experience with others.

The more I shared, the more people started lighting up with interest. And everyone could see that the third part of the formula ("connect") was what completed the circle, producing the experience of oneness for which each of us—for which all of *life*—yearns. People started asking me *how* to *Soulcialize,* and what it was exactly that they were supposed to *remember how to be?*

I discovered that there really was no one answer. I tried saying things like *being your true self* or *living from your Soul,* but after seeing one too many glazed over faces, I realized that those answers didn't seem to mean enough to most people. They seemed to be "just words," and people couldn't get close enough to what it "looked like" to do those things.

Still, people saw changes in me, and friends began asking me for advice. And when I put the *Soulcialize* ideas online, strangers started e-mailing me, wanting my observations and input on their lives. These were people really reaching out to me for some solid guidance, and I knew those bullet-point answers or hazily-worded replies would let them down profoundly.

This all inspired me to sit down and earnestly ask myself what it was that I actually *did* do to activate what I called *Soulcializing*. Headlines started coming to me, so I jotted them down quickly, and noticed that they actually rolled out into sequential steps.

That's when I got a little hung up on things, because I don't care for the word "step"— and the thought of me "giving" someone steps by which to live their life makes me very uneasy—so I decided to share them as *guides*. Not instructions, but rather, soft suggestions that I believe will lead you to the same place of freedom that I found through *Soulcializing*.

Here are the things that came to me:

The Five Guides for Soulcializing

1. Willingness

2. Vulnerability

3. Gratitude

4. Intention

5. Presence

Let's take a look at them, one-by-one.

*Your Soul Mission—
should you choose to accept it . . .*

* The next time you go out, take a moment to check-in with yourself before entering the new space. Briefly connect with yourself and consciously become present with your personal energy and what you are feeling.

* Take a survey of the cloaks you have caught yourself wearing in the past week alone (if any). Have you found yourself disguised as:

  a) Being busy when you're not, because you don't feel like interacting with others?

  b) Knowing something that you don't really know, but are pretending that you do?

  c) Feeling cheerful when you're not?

  d) Having more money than you actually have?

e) Someone who imagines they are more important than others?

Journal your findings and express your feelings around them. Are you surprised at the cloaks that you wear as you become more conscious of them? Are you angry, sad, embarrassed, delighted, or eager to change?

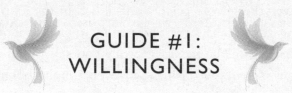

Chapter 13

GUIDE #1: WILLINGNESS

Opening up to our True Selves with others and to life isn't as easy for some as it is for others, but it can be made easy for all of us when we utilize the first Guide to *Soulcializing:* Willingness.

Having the desire and the consent of your heart for more connection as you move through life doesn't guarantee that things will go smoothly, but any choice or action that starts with willingness undeniably has a better chance for success, because it's born from a place of energetic harmony. It begins by flowing *with* the current, whereas being unwilling and resistant is starting out *against* the current.

This may have never crossed your mind, but all of the experiences in your life are created from your level of willingness in things, big and small. Everything from getting out of bed in the morning, taking a shower, and eating, to calling about that job in the paper, allowing yourself to fall in love, starting a business, or even simply looking someone in the eyes.

Why, then, is it sometimes so hard to be willing? And what causes one person to be "more willing" than another?

In most cases, the root of willingness in each of us is driven from our idea about who we are and how we came to be that way. And more often than not, our idea about who we are and how we came to be that way is largely determined by a past experience or behavior that produced either love or pain, reward or punishment.

When we're faced with decisions of any kind (*even the decision to be willing*), we subconsciously weigh what we're considering by revisiting previous experiences and learned information, then comparing the probabilities of the same outcome in the current situation. It's sort of like a personal Willingness Meter that automatically pre-sets our level of willingness around a decision by using our past experiences to determine what we presently consider to be easy or difficult.

This is much like our Default, in that we are pulling resources from the past to determine our future response. The difference between the two is that our Default is an instant and unconscious feeling or reaction, whereas our Willingness Meter is a *conscious* response that was produce by our weighing the likelihood of a future outcome based on the results of a similar past experience.

This idea of a Willingness Meter is not a technique for how to *find* willingness, but rather, an observation on how most of us habitually gauge what the value of our full and open participation in life will be (physically, emotionally, intellectually) based solely on what we think the outcome *may* be—all of which is projected from our past experience of the outcomes that similar decisions have created.

Each one of us exhibits willingness every day throughout the day, but it shows up differently for everyone because we each have a unique Willingness Meter.

For someone who is depressed, having the willingness to start the day and get out of bed in the morning can be a big deal, while for others the idea of "willingness" may never even cross their mind as they swing back the covers in the morning.

For an elderly person, finding the willingness to exert the energy to shower every day can become more and more difficult, while others don't give it a second thought as they reach for the faucet.

And for an anorexic, having the willingness to let go of the reigns and eat is terrifying, while others wouldn't hesitate to meander into the kitchen when hungry.

It's clear, then, that . . .

All willingness is not created equal.

Willingness Meter

Trying to measure how "willing" it makes sense for us to be in any circumstance or situation is an instinctual part of our behavior. The mind is just doing its job by looking out for what it considers to be our best interests and protecting our well-being. The glitch, however, is that if we're always creating our next decision based on the outcome of a past decision, we're living with a self-created sense of limitation.

The definition of "create" is: *to cause to come into being, as something unique that would not naturally evolve or that is not made by ordinary processes.* If we're going to sincerely and organically "create" anything, why wouldn't we create it through a fresh start, a new way, or an open road, as the definition states.

I'm not suggesting that we all get our memories zapped, or even that we try to suppress them. I'm simply proposing that we experience and respond to life from the clarity of the present moment. If this is how we approached life—with willingness e x p a n d e d—then there would be little hesitation or resistance; there would simply be *this way* or *that way*. Decisions would be made from a place deeper and far more trustworthy than our gut-level reaction to our mind's memories. Namely, they would be made from our Soul.

None of this should be construed to mean that we have to be willing to do almost *anything*. There's no reason to feel locked inside some Willingness Quotient that may not support your next highest good. This is about simply being open to seeing that all that past determination-gauging stuff doesn't serve its purpose in keeping us safe and providing us with a general sense of navigation in life, because most of it is our story.

When we can recognize our story and not define ourselves by it, then we can detach from it, not allowing it to determine our next course of action. We can turn off the personal Willingness Meter within, relating to it as a separate piece of luggage, swinging it off our back and gently placing it on the ground. Then our load is lightened, and willingness is born from a place of freedom and trust in our Soul, not from our past experiences.

By nature, our lower thoughts want us to believe that the unknown is something to fear, but whoever said that the unknown is unsafe or something to be scared of? For all we know, it could be more harmful to sit in our comfort zone than it is to venture out and explore.

Think about it—what if the cavemen never left their caves? Willingness is not only a means of finding opportunity, but is very often the catalyst itself that *creates* opportunity. When we agree to move forward into the unknown like this, we are demonstrating willingness. This is courage, activated. Suddenly the vast horizon isn't feared as the unknown, but rather, seen as an enticing destination.

A Three-Way Agreement

There are two types of willingness: Instinctual Willingness and Intentional Willingness. Instinctual Willingness stems from the Soul and is rooted with deep-seeded courage. It's the unexplained knowing, the spontaneous reaction of "Yes." Intentional Willingness stems from the mind. It's the mind's decision to ignore any low reading on our Willingness Meter and *do it anyway*.

Both Instinctual and Intentional Willingness are powered by courage; one is unconscious (that is, from outside the mind; from the Soul directly) and the other is conscious (from inside the mind, having invited the Soul *in*).

Whether it's instinctual or intentional, having willingness around something (especially around *Soulcializing*) is like your Soul agreeing with your mind and body at the same time. Almost as though all three are energetically in a huddle on the same team, stacking their hands upon one another, then throwing them in the air, saying, *"Yes!"* in unison.

Even if the agreement isn't quite that enthusiastic, there's a sense that everyone in your team is onboard with the next move (*"Okay, let's do this! I'll try. I'm ready."*). And that's all that willingness takes—for even if you are willing to be willing, you are being willing.

We are always in a position to choose one thing or another—one path, one way, one idea, a partner, a plan, an action. We are either doing this or that, being this or that. This is creation, our most joyous gift: the freedom to choose *when* and *how much* of *what* we would like to experience.

Life is a constant process of decision-making. We are the ones creating many aspects of our lives from a blank slate. Even if we're following instructions from an employer, advice of a friend, or guidelines from a book, it is always *our* decision, *our* choice, and *our* willingness in the long run, to go this way or that way.

Some people are afraid to be willing because they think it makes them too vulnerable. Yet Soul Courage is what makes it much easier *to step into* vulnerability.

Your Soul Mission— should you choose to accept it ...

* Think about your personal Willingness Meter and notice how big of an influence it has on your current willingness around new opportunities and experiences. Take note in your Soul Courage Journal of any specific references from the past that you find yourself consistently using to support your decision-making process now. Through your journal writing, examine the feelings that you have around those past experiences and notice if the feelings are supporting or not supporting you in making present moment decisions. Make your future decisions accordingly.

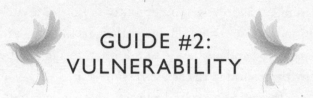

Chapter 14

GUIDE #2:
VULNERABILITY

You may have heard it said that vulnerability is the new power. I'm not particularly a fan of the word power—to me it feels a bit manipulative—but I would definitely agree that vulnerability is *powerful*. And when it's shared authentically (versus being used to gain something), the end result is *extremely* powerful. If I could sing a message from the mountaintop for everyone to hear, I would say:

"Vulnerability is Freedom!
Vulnerability is *the Way*."

By "being vulnerable," I'm not suggesting that you wear your heart on your sleeve and reveal your deepest thoughts and emotions to everyone who crosses your path, or that you cry at any given moment, sharing your personal feelings through mini-breakdowns. Vulnerability is not an invitation to "lose it" at will, but rather, to find it. Find your true and authentic self. Find it, feel it, and be softly grounded in the expression of it.

It would be a mistake to assume that being vulnerable is the same as being emotionally unstable. Being emotionally unstable means that you are unsteady and wavering in your feelings, and that a minor occurrence could trigger an inappropriate response involving extreme emotions.

Vulnerability, on the other hand, broadly means being emotionally accessible, unguarded, unprotected with others and yourself. The act of feeling, itself, is classified as being vulnerable because as we discussed before, we don't know where our feelings are going take us.

A daily example of low-level vulnerability is how many of us feel when we ask questions. Even a simple question, such as: "Do you know how to get to the post office?" The very asking of any question announces to all that we do not have the answer ourselves. This can make some people feel vulnerable (some men, in particular, can find it difficult to even stop a car to ask for directions).

When others ask me how they can become vulnerable, they're frequently surprised by my answer. *"You're being vulnerable right now by asking the question,"* I reply, then remind them with a smile: *"You are always vulnerable. That's your natural state of being. It's part of who you are with every breath you take."*

You may not think of yourself this way— probably because it makes you *feel vulnerable* to think of yourself this way! Yet the fact is that life itself is unpredictable and uncertain, even as we rely on it to be there. Every night we set our alarm with the expectation that life will greet us the next day. The very fact that *we rely on the unknown* makes us all vulnerable at some level.

Unconsciously and at a very deep level we have befriended uncertainty, and we continue to live with the unknown *every . . . single . . . day*. I'd say that keeps vulnerability flowing through our blood, for sure.

That being said, it's still uncomfortable for most people to even wrap their mind around the concept that vulnerability is good for you, let alone that they would benefit from *deliberately* allowing themselves to be vulnerable. They get uneasy at the thought of it and begin to challenge the idea.

It takes a lot of courage and awareness to let your guard down and drop into vulnerability. Interestingly enough, though, we've been told the exact opposite for decades: that being vulnerable is not a mark of courage, but is a sign of being weak, pathetic, and child-like.

We've been told that to be successful, respected, seen and heard (and even sexy), our demeanor must be confident, stoic, and even a bit arrogant. This has led to some of us feeling that we actually need to be pretentious, maintaining a facade that produces the impression that we're extremely capable in every situation (remember those cloaks?).

We've been taught that the way to do this is to hide our feelings as they arise and *"fake it 'til you make it,"* acting as if we are calm, cool, and have everything under control at all times.

And guess what? Everything *has* been "under control." From the time we were toddlers all the way through adulthood many of us have learned to control every feeling our hearts have experienced that was either too high or too low, so that they would appear *nice and even* to our "audience." It's the whole Middle Ground preference we were discussing earlier, that most people reside in to avoid feeling deeply.

We were trained and coached to: *Keep quiet. Stop crying. Calm down. Let it roll off your back. Don't get too excited.* We've even developed a reference for others who do this with such ease. We say, *"You're cool!"*

Somewhere along the way humanity learned to value those who hide their true selves, and we've been passing that value system down generation after generation. We thought we were teaching our offspring something good when, in fact, we've had it all backward. The more open and real we are with others and ourselves, the more we reflect genuine confidence and self-assurance. Pretending that we're something we are not is what makes us truly look child-like, if not downright cowardly.

While no one wants to look that way, we are still reluctant to consciously befriend vulnerability, largely *because* we've been taught that vulnerability is a weakness. Our mind tells us that this isn't a character trait of ours that we want others to know about. We're not proud to have it seen pouring from our hearts.

But when we understand that vulnerability is the natural state of every human being, we can let go of our need to *hide* this aspect of ourselves. Then the question switches from *how to become* more vulnerable, to *what relationship we have* with our vulnerability. And, more importantly, is that relationship supporting our highest good?

Many of us probably haven't ever thought about having a relationship with ourselves, much less having a relationship with individual *aspects* of ourselves—and we've surely never thought about *what kind* of relationship we have with *each* aspect, such as our vulnerability.

Yet taking a closer look at yourself in this way often instills a sense of compassion for all aspects of "you"—and ultimately bridges into a deeper understanding of yourself. Identifying what relationship we have with vulnerability also allows us to determine if that relationship itself is encouraging our vulnerability to live openly and abundantly in our life—which we want, because that will reawaken even *greater* vulnerability in ourselves.

Discovering Your
Relationship with Vulnerability

The quickest way to discover what relationship you have with vulnerability (as well as any other individual aspect of yourself) is to—you guessed it—take note of how you feel when you're experiencing vulnerability.

Having been vulnerable enough to express your feeling in a truthful way (by something as simple as the look on your face, or the way you carry yourself— to say nothing about actually revealing verbally something important about yourself), do you feel positive in the aftermath, or do you wish you had never done it?

Are you angry? Are you sad? Are you embarrassed, ashamed, or disgusted? Do you feel relieved, free, and open? Are you humbled? Are you disappointed in yourself? Do you feel exposed and frightened? Are you delighted?

This feeling, whatever it is, will reveal to you how it is that you relate to vulnerability deep inside, ultimately defining the relationship that you have created with vulnerability thus far.

Should we discover that our relationship with vulnerability is inhibiting us in some way, this process gives us an opportunity to recreate that relationship so that we not only feel safe with it, but also are proud of it. By pulling it out from the back room and bringing it forward in our daily life, we see and feel its value as we notice our relationships being enriched.

This is exactly what our Soul came here to experience: Feel-Express-Connect. And the benefits of this far surpass any underlying desire to appear capable and confident, or to be respected and accepted.

So how, then, does one actually "be" vulnerable? Where do you start?

Well, you'll be relieved to know that you've already started. That's right. Years and years ago. We are all delivered to life as vulnerable beings at birth. No doubt that is why babies are so appealing to us because, in a sense, they are pure vulnerability.

But the relationship we have with vulnerability changes through the years. We start off being wide open and slowly shift, putting defenses into place in reaction to our personal experiences as we were taught (by others and by life itself) what is "right" and "wrong," what is "good" and "bad."

Yet as much as we have shifted and changed through the years, some degree of vulnerability still exists in everyone. It will always exist in us, which is a good thing, because it's a key to our humanity itself. Without at least a little bit of vulnerability we would all be robots, like the character Data in Star Trek, unable to feel anything about anything.

If you find that your present relationship with vulnerability does not usually make you happy, yet deliberately choose to feel vulnerable in spite of that, you are consciously saying to yourself that what your vulnerability revealed to you, or others about you, is nothing to be afraid of, ashamed of, or embarrassed about. You've taken the power away from the thought that those emotions can hurt you in some way. Used in this way, the process of consciously choosing vulnerability empowers you, rather than making you feel as if you were a victim of having had a vulnerable moment.

You will watch as you eagerly peel back the layers of protection (Resistance Techniques, Defaults, cloaks, etc.) under which your vulnerability had been hiding, and intentionally make it as big and natural a part of your experience as it was when you were young.

This transition from being hesitant to be vulnerable to being *eager* to be vulnerable will utterly transform you, and will forever alter your relationship with others for the better.

Most people don't know this, of course. Which is why it takes Soul Courage to discover it.

The Hidden Gift of Vulnerability

When vulnerability is experienced as an adult, you will see that you are in actuality *invulnerable*. The *intentional* act of you telling, living, and speaking your truth renders you free from feeling that you have to *protect yourself* from being really seen and really known. And freedom from the need for protection is the *definition* of invulnerability.

The more you relax into vulnerability and become comfortable functioning from that place, the more you'll realize this. You will then begin to experience yourself in a new way, and enjoy living in such a genuine place that it will almost feel as if you've come out of hiding.

Before you know it, you won't be picking and choosing times to "be" vulnerable. Rather, you'll be operating from a place that is *always* vulnerable, on purpose. This will heighten your overall awareness, showing you clearly how often you rejected yourself in the past by reaching for a distraction or protective cloak.

When you know that distractions and protections are no longer needed the tide will have turned. Now vulnerability will feel like home, and all of those exhausting masks, which you thought brought you the comfort of protection, will actually be *un*comfortable.

A small caution: As you find yourself living with vulnerability on a more consistent basis, it is possible that you may initially feel as if your mind is betraying you by dispensing with its safety mechanisms and opting for self-exposure. But don't be fooled . . . this is really a magic moment, a Soul kiss, as you realize that it's the exact opposite.

Now you've become so comfortable being vulnerable that you don't even feel vulnerable. And—to make the point again—you aren't. You are *invulnerable*, unable to be coaxed back over to the other side where you thought you needed to protect yourself. Uninhibited emotionally. You'll feel impenetrable—because you've revealed your true self and your true feelings on your own, before being "found out" by others, and you now express your truth willingly.

Feeling Your Way Back Into Invulnerability

Now that you know how to identify what relationship you have with your vulnerability and *why* to open to full vulnerability once again, let's look at *how*. There are two ways to experience the hidden gift of vulnerability:

1. Be reactive and wait for life to show it to you *(the hard way)*.

2. Be proactive and reveal it to yourself *(can be unnerving, but isn't hard)*.

Most people choose number one without thinking about it, mainly because they *haven't* thought about it. They're living life by rote, due to their lack of awareness of the hidden gift of vulnerability, or to their uneasiness about the whole topic, as we spoke of earlier, which has produced a lack of interest. Yet you are reading this right now, so I suspect that *you're* ready to be proactive in turning vulnerability into invulnerability through the process of *Soulcializing*.

Actually, *it* will reveal itself to *you*. Because (let me say once again, for emphasis) as you notice and expose your vulnerabilities, you cannot help but see that true invulnerability comes with doing so.

Sometimes when we're trying to get to a place of vulnerability we don't know where to start. In my experience there are some tools that can be helpful in building enough vulnerability to experience oneself as being invulnerable: Trust, Intuition, Ego, and Authenticity.

Trust

Being vulnerable calls on us to trust. Trust that we'll be okay if we *allow ourselves* to be vulnerable. But here again is a Catch 22: You can't get there without going there, yet you must trust that going there will get you there.

The quickest way to get there?

No surprise . . . Soul Courage.

By uniting with the Soul (using our handy formula of Feel-Express-Connect) you move away from the protections and devices of the mind, allowing fear to drop away by bringing "knowing" to the surface. It is the knowing of the Soul that makes it possible for you to feel safe enough to trust.

As you engage your Soul in supporting you in life—through *Soulitude*, *Soulrender*, and this process of *Soulcializing* we are now describing—you will eventually gravitate towards trust more, viewing it as a reflection of being loyal to yourself.

Your Soul is always grounded behind-the-scenes, knowing and believing in the totality of who you are, and offering complete and utter support, aware that you cannot be hurt or damaged in any way.

This experience of deep peace, expanded knowing and eternal safety is what arises through teaming up with your Soul, which moves you seamlessly into trust. By *trusting in this process* you are affirming your Soul's existence, which honors yourself at the highest level.

Your Soul will never leave you, it cannot leave you. Not because it doesn't have a choice, but because you *are* its choice. It chose you. It *is* you. You and your Soul are one. When you are deeply aware of yourself you will know this to be true, and you will forever trust yourself to be vulnerable.

By mentally taking the idea of trusting yourself and seeing it as an accomplishment when you do, it will not only come more naturally, but also empower you by creating the ambition to do it more often.

Deliberate action is a *direct demonstration* of trust. It says that you trust the outcome of your actions. On the occasion that you find yourself uneasy with vulnerability, try this quick *deliberate* exercise to produce Trust—reminding yourself once again that trust is a doorway to vulnerability.

First, let yourself to feel into any distrust that may be present regarding what you think will happen if you become vulnerable. Feel this enough to really experience the discomfort of it. This will heighten your sensitivity to the truth, inviting you to then be 100 percent honest with yourself about how much of what you think will happen is real, and how much of it is imagined (taking an honest look of any situation is part of a wonderful strategy introduced by Byron Katie in her book, *Loving What Is*).

If you pay close attention, you will literally feel yourself drop out of your mind and into your heart. The actual physical feeling in your body will shift from tension and uneasiness to surrender and peace. You will realize with a newfound certainty that it's your only thoughts, as opposed to the real you that cannot to be trusted.

Intuition

Another tool that helps us to move into vulnerability comfortably is our intuition. Stop looking elsewhere to find a reason to trust. So often we look outside ourselves for guidance and protection, when all the while we carry it within. Our innate sense of knowing is deeply *under*rated, and that is why we don't trust it. Ironically, though, the most trustworthy way to build vulnerability is *through* that innate sense of knowing.

The *reason* that we don't always trust our intuition is that we don't fully understand it, and our lack of understanding around it decreases our faith in it. In fact, many people don't really believe it exists at all. But it does. And *you* know this, *intuitively*.

We've all had the experience of a strong hunch, a gut reaction, or a natural instinct—a surge of knowingness that expands past our ordinary thoughts. Maybe we get goose bumps to alert us, a twisted tummy, or tingle in our chest (more on this later). Whatever the sign, it produces an inexplicable feeling that resonates with us beyond our mind, into our body, having emerged from our Soul.

Intuition, like Soul Courage, is with us all of the time. Mostly, though, we wait until we need it before we begin to look for it. And interestingly enough, we put our fate in the hands of others *first,* draining resources such as family, friends, the Internet, even psychics—then lastly crawling back to the most reliable resource for our life, *us,* and resorting to going within for the direction we seek.

It's been said that we can "tap into" our intuition, which is another way of saying that we can bring it forth upon command. This idea implies that our intuition is with us all of the time and that we can pick and choose when to "use" it. But if it *were* with us all the time, why wouldn't we desire to *live with it and through it,* rather than wait until we need it, to call it forth? Presumably because, as mentioned above, we don't fully understand it, therefore we don't hold that as a real option.

I looked up the definition of intuition and literally chuckled out loud when I read some of the explanations.

Intuition: {in-too-*ish*-uh, n} *noun*
"A natural ability or power that makes
it possible to know something without
any proof or evidence." —*Merriam-Webster*

"A phenomenon of the mind; the ability
to acquire knowledge without inference
or the use of reason." —*Wikipedia*

What I found amusing about these definitions is that they seem to suggest that our intuition is a phenomenon or unique ability. Yet it's not about tapping into your higher powers or "channeling" information from another entity. Those things would all suggest that there's distance and separation between you and your intuition . . . and there is not. The actual name itself, *in-tuition,* carries the clear and irrefutable inference that we are receiving our very own teachings from deep within: Our inner schooling.

But *what* is schooling us from inside? There's no denying that *something* continues to propel us to take one direction over the other. In fact, that's even how we describe things to friends when they ask what prompted our decision. We say, "I can't explain. *Something* just told me to do it!"

My hunch is that "this something" is *us*. Not our body, not our mind, not even our spirit, but rather the fusion of all three. If this were true, then when we are trusting and following our intuition, we are, in fact, *listening to our Soul.*

Living Through Intuition

I distinctively remember the feeling of my intuition being magnified when I was released from the hospital's eating disorder unit. It was as if everything inside me was finally open for business. The Clarity Switch was turned on high, and initially it actually did feel as if I had special powers—or at least an elevated awareness of everything that was happening around me—because it was such a contrast to my current numb and fuzzy perception.

Somehow the vulnerabilities I felt from being in the hospital allowed me to drop into trust around who I really was and why I was here on this planet. I felt a new kinship with my Soul in a way I had never once imagined I could, in all of my stargazing years. But soon, my mind began challenging me with questions like, "Wait a minute, if intuition is actually the Soul speaking, why don't I hear it more often? Why doesn't it speak in more clear and concise ways? And what's up with having to pray, meditate, and plead just to connect with the Soul, especially during crucial times?"

I still find myself asking these questions when I'm frustrated or in my fear. But angst and faith are like oil and water, they each vibrate at such completely different levels that it's impossible for them to co-exist for long. One of the two eventually gets pushed out, and more often than not, it's faith.

As you know, faith doesn't exist unless you believe that it does (since the entire premise of faith is believing), so here we are again, standing at the corner of that good old Catch 22: You can't have faith unless you believe there is faith to have, and you don't believe there is faith to have unless you have faith. Feeling a deep belief in anything is what actually gives birth *to it* in our experience. This is especially true of Intuition, and of the Soul.

The more we believe our Soul speaks through intuition, the more aware we become of the Soul's presence, and we find ourselves open to receiving messages more clearly. It's not about "tapping into" this relationship with the Soul, but about bringing this relationship into the *forefront* of our daily lives.

We can begin to live *through* intuition more by increasing our awareness of it, using our feeling decoder, our body. By identifying the physical symptoms we experience in correlation to the emotions we're feeling, we are learning to "hear" the messages of our Soul through intuition.

For example, when your tummy feels funny, don't just think to yourself, "My stomach feels strange." Take an extra step to pause and use your feeling decoder (aka, your body) to notice if it is a bellyache (which your previous experience may correlate to nervousness), butterflies (could be excitement) or sharp cramps (could be fear)—as each represents a different emotion in every individual, giving everyone a custom-made message that corresponds to how their body and emotions intuitively interact.

When you become familiar enough with how your physical symptoms relate to and telegraph your instinct, you can start living *through* your intuition, as if it were your personal doorway to inner guidance. Because it is.

Living through your intuition like this supports you in making decisions that are in your highest good, guiding you along the way like an internal lighthouse.

When we ignore our intuition altogether we are shifting ourselves into the position of being a guest in our own home. This usually only happens when we don't know better, don't trust ourselves, or if our mind and ego start talking us out of what we know to be true inside.

Vulnerability and the Ego

As previously discussed, the challenge for so many people around vulnerability and trust is letting go of the way they *think* they are "supposed" to be. Letting go of worry around what they may look like if they actually reveal the inside of themselves. Letting go of concern around what others think about them. In other words, confronting ego.

Ego is a natural part of who we are, a part of our overall mind that is neither something to be ashamed of nor disposed of. In fact, it plays a very important role in how we navigate life and ultimately experience our True Self.

Although it sounds totally villainess upon first reflection, the ego's main job of seducing us into believing that we are separate from one another actually has a beneficial purpose.

In order to feel and experience the joy of oneness (which is our natural state and the Ultimate Reality), ego steps in to create the *illusion* that we are separate, thus providing us with a platform upon which we can create and express our individuality. With this illusion of separateness firmly embraced, we are able to distinguish differences and opposites—in contrast to which our individuality may be expressed and experienced.

Our True Self (Soul) is one step ahead of our ego (of course), and knows that there's no such thing as separation. The challenge is that while the Soul *knows* this, it does not have the actual *experience* of oneness, and this is the very experience it sought when it embraced physicality—a point made at the outset of this book. There it was said that the Soul cannot *feel* oneness in the metaphysical realm, because it has known nothing *but* oneness.

Yet oneness cannot even be experienced in the physical realm without the contrast of it's opposite showing up—so our ego instills in us the illusion of separation (which is possible only in the physical), allowing the Soul to now *experience*, and not just "know," the opposite of separation: oneness. If the illusion of separation were not suggested by our ego in this physical life, the state of being eternally one would not be able to be experienced.

The ego's job is to ignite your desire to be the highest version of yourself (that which is one with everyone, on both the metaphysical and physical plane), but when the mind isn't listening to the Soul, it doesn't understand what the Soul is doing. Ego all by itself certainly doesn't know—it's just an energy trying to get you where you want to go. The danger of our ego is that somewhere along the way in our life it begins to think so highly of itself that it creates an identity of its own. It starts to disregard the body and the mind *and the Soul*—all three—thinking that it knows what's best for us.

At almost any point in time you can find ego sitting in the audience in the theater of the mind, trying to seduce us into ideas of not just *separation*, but also *superiority*, which must then seek self-protection and express righteousness.

And the idea of our superiority is *so* seductive that, if we're not careful, we might inadvertently hand over the reins to ego and forget who we

really are (one with everyone—and so, not supe-
rior at all).

Here's where things get interesting, here's
where everything ties together: The more we are
in a place of invulnerability, the shorter the leash is
on the ego. This gives it enough elbowroom to do
its job, but not excessive slack for it to run amok.
When we have become so comfortable with vulnerability that we are invulnerable, this invulnerability takes the power away from the ego that's
gotten out-of-control.

Mind Chatter

Like a little monkey on a scooter peeling corners
around the back of our mind, our thoughts often
create "mind chatter." It can take us to places where
we never dreamed we'd go. And, it can impede our
efforts to produce or experience invulnerability,
talking us right out of it if we aren't careful.

Notice, though, that when you actually stop and
become aware of this chatter, it seems to drop away.
Falls right off the bone. Right there is the golden
moment (another Soul kiss) when the "monkey
mind" has left, opening the space for far more

wonderful input from your Soul. There, in that moment, floats a pocket of silence in your mind.

To feel this sensation, this gift, relish these golden moments when they surface by *feeling into* the silence and past its *seemingly* empty space, instead of quickly filling the pockets of silence with anything to comfort the uncomfortable. This is where the freedom to open to your highest thoughts lives.

The more often you feel *into* the silence, the more aware you will become of how often the ongoing white noise of the mind chatter is running behind the scenes, and the more you will want it to go away, so that you can spend time with "you."

Authenticity

Being authentic is the largest aspect of vulnerability—and, in fact, one of the largest aspects of life and true living. This is why it's considered non-negotiable when *Soulcializing*.

The only way that we can allow ourselves to be vulnerable, even in the slightest bit, is if we are completely authentic with ourselves *first*. It's not possible to be vulnerable without being authentic, and it's not possible to be authentic without being vulnerable; one cannot exist without the other. Even when we are alone—we can't actually feel vulnerable unless we are being truly genuine with ourselves.

The more time goes by, the more it becomes apparent that embracing our authenticity is a prerequisite for ultimate self-discovery and inner growth. If we can't be real with ourselves, how can we possibly feel comfortable enough to suddenly show up in our purest form with others—let alone with complete strangers?

When we let our guard down and reveal our authentic nature with others, it's like handing them a gift. Being authentic in the presence of others is like an energetic invitation for others to meet you at the same vibrational level. This is the whole premise of *Soulcializing*, as said earlier. It's not that you are giving other people permission to "come out" from behind any cloak they may have on, you are energetically encouraging their authenticity from the start so that they don't even have the desire to put *on* a cloak.

Getting Comfortable in Your Own Skin

The best way to move into authenticity with ease is to roll up your sleeves and get comfortable in your own skin. No one even has to be around for this to start, it's just about you being comfortable with yourself. The more comfortable you become with yourself, the more it becomes a part of how you project yourself outwardly to the world.

But how do you get *that* comfortable with yourself? Sure, maybe when you're completely alone and relaxed, you're comfortable with who you are. This may be true even when you're around your family (although for many people *that's* not even a "given" most of the time). Yet how are we to magically produce a feeling of great comfort "on demand" when others are around?

To become comfortable in your skin, you should be familiar with the skin that you want to be comfortable in, which means you should have a good idea of every aspect of your personality, yours likes and dislikes, your desires and goals—everything about you that is important and feels like your genuine self.

You may have already done some past reflection of your own, and feel pretty solid in knowing who you are, with a good sense of your personal energy. Now it's time to own that. Hold that so securely as your own that it's yours to call on wherever and whenever you want. While you're at it, don't take yourself too seriously. Seriously, don't do it. There's just no reason to do so.

As adults we certainly have to take care of serious matters and act accordingly, but if we allow the weight of seriousness to conduct our livelihood we're robbing ourselves and others of the luxury of lightheartedness, and slowly stripping joy from our spirit. All of which ages us emotionally, spiritually, and, yes, even physically, by the way. It also keeps others at a distance by nonverbally conveying that they need to "stay in line" when they are in our company.

Objectively, it could be argued that someone who is overly serious is operating with an unconscious desire to be seen as important, smart, special, in charge, etc. Conversely, it might be said that someone who is always joking around and acting out, has a subconscious, underlying desire to be seen as funny, different, clever, special, etc.

Either one, when out of balance, becomes a cloak at some level and keeps others at arm's length, which is far from being comfortable in your skin. One of the goals of *Soulcializing* is to find the "genuine" in ourselves again, and then to feel comfortable sharing that with others and ourselves.

Let Your Freak Flag Fly

Some of us may remember the term "Freak Flag" from the 70s, but what does it actually mean? My understanding is that this phrase originated as an expression from the hippies that means to let your hair flow freely—or, in other words, to defy all means of "being normal" and controlled.

The definition has expanded through the years into one that now generally means *be yourself, utterly and completely—with no embarrassment or apologies—* stripping yourself of any need to obey the rules and letting your quirky self out to play. Not only when you're alone and it feels safe to do so, but as an expression of who you are. It means to liberate yourself at the level where there are no holds barred or worries about what others may think.

Nobody is suggesting that you take your clothes off and dance on bar tops, or engage in other ridiculous and inane acts of defiance (not every day, that is), but rather, simply release and express the joyous, child-like freedom within you. Once you find your Freak Flag, wave it in the wind like a kite, in celebration of it finally being unfurled. The celebration is not the finding of it, but the embracing of it fully as part of who you are.

Here's an interesting tidbit about the Freak Flag: when it does take flight, it not only reveals a vulnerable side of you, but also reveals that you're comfortable with that vulnerable side of you, and that you don't hesitate to reveal yourself by worrying about what others may think.

One of the quickest ways to get comfortable in your skin is to start flying your flag at home. Get nice and snuggled up with the silly side of you and share it with the walls. Sing a little. Crack jokes. Maybe even dance.

The more comfortable you are letting your personality out when you're alone, the more it will fill you up and become a natural part of your expression when you are out. Then start sharing it with your family or close friends and watch as they open up and join you, now that they know it's safe, letting their Freak Flag out to play, too!

Some people understand this intuitively and demonstrate it naturally throughout their life. My father is one of these people. He knows how to have fun when he is by himself or with others. He delights in bringing humor and a sense of lightness to many moments.

One of the dear things he used to do, as he drove somewhere with my sister and I when we were little girls, was to spontaneously repeat the last sentence he spoke, over and over like a robot. It wasn't until the third or fourth rollout that we realized what he was doing. It was a little game that we played, and we knew that he would not stop until one of us leaned over and squeezed his nose—a form of "rewiring" that repaired the robot's malfunction.

After one of us pinched his nose, he would just continue the sentence as if nothing ever happened.

Often he would then take a surprise detour into the drive-through at McDonald's. We knew immediately what he was going to do: order milk-shakes for us and use an old man voice to bring a laugh to the checkout girl. He knew that she would be expecting someone really old to show up when the car pulled around. Then he would speak in his regular voice and watch her confusion.

It was always a no-fail game that still works to this day—as I discovered recently when we were out running errands one afternoon and he pulled the same old stunt. We sipped on our milkshakes and joked about how surprised we were that the trick still actually worked, since he now really *is* older and fully gray. I guess the clerk was expecting someone to look even older than he looks, because she smiled as he spoke in his normal voice . . . or maybe she was simply delighted to see someone having fun, and sharing it so openly.

The sweet thing about this ride with Dad wasn't that it was a barrel of fun or that I got to drink a McDonald's milkshake for the first time in twenty-plus years, but that he instantly connected us through a shared memory of how freely he felt to entertain himself and others by letting loose and being comfortable in his own skin doing so.

Sharing your silliest, most real and goofy self is a beautiful way to *Soulcialize* with your family and friends—and for that matter, even with complete strangers.

Imagine how it would increase the connectedness and hope in our hearts if we did this with *at least* one person a day—even if that person was our self. This can be amazingly healing when such moments are fueled by love and joy.

Whether your Freak Flag is out and flying high like a kite or you're just getting it strung up, don't forget that it exists. Celebrating the unique things that make you, *you*, is a no-fail way to get comfortable in your skin. And being comfortable in your skin, as I have repeatedly said, supports you in expressing openly, which is a pillar of *Soulcializing*.

Generosity

As you freely share your energetic self and reveal the genuine "inside you" with yourself, without hesitation, your mind won't even have the chance to step in and misrepresent you. Yes! You've found your way back to your relaxed, authentic, down-to-earth self, and now the best part awaits. Now you get to share all of that awesomeness with others! (No sense in keeping it to yourself.)

Most of the time we walk around in our own world, filling our minds with worries and the current "to do" list. When we're out and about, we may even tell ourselves things such as, "I'm busy, and I just don't have time to be friendly." But that's usually an excuse we make to ourselves in order to justify staying in our comfort zone.

When we avoid others, we are not only depriving ourselves of what they have to offer, but also depriving them of the gift of who we are. When we are generous with our accessibility and authentic energy, we open others and ourselves up to new experiences.

The Wean and Lean

Approaching vulnerability in a way *that works* takes a bit of finesse. "Requiring" something of ourselves gets us way fewer results than simply inviting ourselves to a new idea, feeling, or thought.

The dynamic of not wanting to be pushed into something, but at the same time wanting to get immediate results, is not uncommon. Yet it's more natural and appealing to wean into something new by leaning into it a little more each day.

If we want flowers in our garden to bloom by spring, we know that we must first plant the seeds and tend to them with water and sunshine, nurturing them for some time before we can expect to even see a bud, let alone full extension of their petals and glory.

When exploring your vulnerability, try to tend to the garden of your thoughts. Be kind and try not to make yourself wrong in any way. Don't let your process of discovery be a reprimand or a criticism of how you and vulnerability have thus far interacted in life, but simply an examination of that, and a noticing of whether this has or has not worked to your greatest benefit.

There's been a lot said in this chapter. My wish for you now is that you take your time absorbing all that you've found here—and take even more time implementing it.

Your Soul Mission—
should you choose to accept it . . .

* Think of a few times that you felt vulnerable and look at what you initially thought that vulnerability would rob you of . . . then look what gift that brought to the moment.

* Make a list of five people that you are uncomfortable being vulnerable with and journal the positive things that could happen if you let guard down around them. Pick someone from that list to connect with in a vulnerable way, applying some of the ideas from this chapter.

* Close your eyes right now and ask yourself these two questions without censoring yourself. Write the answers that immediately came to you, in your Soul Courage Journal.

   a) What will my life look like when I'm in full expression?

b) What will my life look like when I support others to live in full expression?

＊ The next time you're with family or close friends, dare to come out and play, sharing generously a little more of your silly self than you may do normally. Watch their reaction and energetically invite them to join in the fun. Notice how the laughter and playfulness brings you closer.

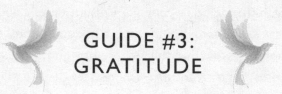

Chapter 15

GUIDE #3: GRATITUDE

Of all the guides in *Soulcializing,* gratitude offers the deepest underlying foundation. That is because gratitude keeps you present, shifting your personal energy and the energy around you.

Appreciating something in the moment establishes that we *are* in that moment. Whether we are the one expressing gratitude or the person receiving another's gratitude, appreciation in the moment establishes presence with all that is, in both people.

By bringing us to *right now*, the exchange of gratitude keeps our mind out of the past and out of the future. This gives us a sense of enormous freedom, allowing us to fully experience and express what we are feeling *now*. This is one of the many ways that gratitude facilitates *Soulcializing*.

Believe it or not, though, feeling and expressing gratitude takes courage. I'm not talking about a casual "Thank you!" when someone opens the door for you, but full on feeling gratitude and expressing it to another, face to face.

This takes courage because to feel gratitude full on is to feel love full on. And the mind often tells us it's dangerous to feel love full on, so we live with an invisible cage around our heart.

When we are the receiver of gratitude, we often don't feel worthy of receiving the gratitude and the love within it, and start to fend it off immediately, or lessen its value, saying, *"Oh, it was nothing."*

Even if we are completely alone and feeling gratitude for something in our life in the privacy of our mind, it's sometimes followed with guilt. The guilt of feeling unworthy of receiving that for which we are grateful, the guilt of feeling that you put another out.

Oddly, it doesn't stop there. We can sometimes feel shame even as we are expressing gratitude to another. This is the shame of somehow feeling defeated and admitting that we were incapable of handling on our own what we are thanking them for. This is why it is difficult for a lot of people to express gratitude verbally or in writing, let alone in person, and actually look the other in the eyes.

But pausing and looking someone in the eyes with sincere appreciation can erase all feelings of inadequacy. It's as though we hit the "re-set" button through the power of Connection. Everything we were carrying—our To Do list, our worries about the future, our preoccupations about the past, and any feeling of unworthiness—is suddenly zapped.

It's as though gratitude has a force of its own, like a beam of light that diminishes everything else around it. Our mind is so attracted to this light that everything around it falls away, and we feel ourselves again. That's how powerful gratitude is. It not only magnetizes us to other people, it magnetizes us to our Soul.

We suddenly feel what's really important, as our "story" disintegrates right in front of our eyes.

Even when we think we're done feeling the gratitude, it still resides within us. If we try to get back to our previous state of mind—the worries, the To Do list, etc.—suddenly we feel much more indifferent about it. We have reset the pins on the bowling alley of life. Something or someone may knock them down again, but we've found the *magic reset button.*

By virtue of gratitude keeping us present, we are lifted out of lower vibrations, if only for the moment. Lower vibrations can be anything from fear and anxiety, or even the story that we may unconsciously carry with us throughout the day (i.e., *"I'm never good enough." "No one ever sees me." "I'm not worthy."*).

You may have had the experience of being afflicted by one of these lower thoughts, and then something wonderful will happen that yanks you out of that vibration and unexpectedly rolls you into a place of joy. One moment you're feeling angst or despair, the next you're feeling an intense appreciation for someone or something.

We see, then, that gratitude isn't just about saying *thank you*. We could say *thank you* until the cows come home and may still not have one iota of gratitude in our hearts, because gratitude is about *feeling* thanks. I'm sure you know this, but what you may not know is how to actually go about *feeling it deliberately.*

Gratitude is generally experienced unpredictably. It's something that just "happens" to you on occasion. Perhaps after you've been given a gift or support from a friend, you've felt your heart open up the same way that it does when you hug someone. It's wonderful when this happens spontaneously, but can be life-changing when you create it intentionally.

How to Feel Gratitude on Purpose

Although we are inclined to think that gratitude is about being grateful for something or someone else, the best place to start creating it on purpose is to be grateful for yourself.

Taking the time to notice and reflect on the things that you are grateful for about *you* puts your mind on the backburner and allows your heart and Soul to step forward. To feel gratitude on purpose, think of the things right now that you have to be grateful for about you.

Even if you are simply appreciating something from your past, the act of feeling thankful about it reminds you of your long-standing existence—and that in itself is a reason to be grateful.

Lacking Lack

With much of society focused on making a financial profit, and the increased acceptance around disposability, humanity has become ever consumed with a case of Not-Enoughness. The days of living simple and being grateful for what we *do* have, have been traded for living lavishly, sometimes beyond our means, and pining for what we don't have.

Much of our daily thinking has been poisoned from the larger thought of lack that there is not enough; that we are not enough, or that things should be a better way. It's no shock, then, to see the rapid decline of gratitude trickle though our species.

Lack of gratitude spawns from the feeling of lack, itself. According to your mind, you are lacking this and lacking that, and pretty soon you become resentful and can only see all that it is you are lacking, which, then, organically produces a lack of gratitude.

But there is a solution, a way to get back to feeling more gratitude for all things. The solution is to abandon the feeling of lack.

The Visual Visit

Operation Lack-Removal starts by staying present with all that you do have, which keeps your mind busy and unable to think about all that you want or think you need. You can instantly become present with all that you have by physically looking at your surroundings. Just glance around the room and consciously take in the beauty around you. Notice that wherever you are, there *is* beauty.

Whether you are simply staring at the grass or the sky, looking at your spouse, your children, your pet, your home, or even looking down at your own hands and feet, your visual visit will ignite your recognition of the wonder of these things, and will fill your heart with gratitude.

If you hear thoughts of lack "at work" in your mind, spouting off the list of all that you "need to be" and "must have" in order to experience happiness, try not to fall prey to the hypnosis by feeling dissatisfied about life in some way (money, relationship, body image, etc.). Instead of being mentally paralyzed by the anguish of wishing things were different—or scrambling to change things and make them "better"—try to catch those thoughts as soon as they appear and blow them out as if they were a flame on a candle. Then bring yourself back to the truth you *choose* by consciously taking a look around the room again to see what *is* there.

This exercise will prove that your thoughts of lack are inaccurate by immediately giving them proof of the opposite. Voluntarily leaving those thoughts of lack and moving into the watcher will empower you, and as you review the treasures in your life, your trust that you will always be taken care of will be affirmed. Gratitude will arise in your heart and you will now *feel* that *"everything is perfect exactly as it is."* Notice that you have always had everything you've needed . . . your being here right now is the proof.

Verbal Acknowledgement

Another way to feel gratitude on purpose is to express it intentionally, and not just spontaneously. And out loud, not just to yourself.

Don't just think about how wonderful something or someone is, share the wealth. And watch as something that may have initially been merely "nice" in your thoughts, then grows in your heart and the hearts of others as you declare your gratitude for it verbally.

This can be unexpectedly enlivening to both the giver and the receiver of gratitude, because people simply don't get enough of it. Everyone wants to be seen, yet some people seem to not have the time, interest, or courage to actually "see" another. The sending of gratitude is almost always a roll-over experience, in that the initial giver of the gratitude sends joy to the receiver, responds joyfully, the energy of which comes back full circle, gifting the original giver with the very essence of what was sent.

You can also express gratitude about something not related to that person, but shared with them directly. If you're expressing gratitude for the weather, for example, the person hearing it still feels uplifted by your words of appreciation, and may even share a light-hearted or happy response—or even engage in a wider conversation with you. *This is what Soulcializing is all about.*

Yet, there doesn't even have to be another person in the space in order for you to acknowledge something verbally. I know you know this, but how often do you actually do it? Acknowledging something verbally to yourself—an animal, nature, or even to the Universe/God of your choice—when no one is around is surprisingly powerful and exhilarating.

The idea of positive affirmations came from this discovery, and I have no doubt that's why they are so popular. There is a magical twist in hearing your own voice appreciate anything with love and gratitude.

There's no need to be embarrassed or afraid that you're going crazy when you acknowledge something out loud. This is simply a more tangible way of revealing the inner truth arising from your Soul.

Acts of Service

An act of service is a very proactive and sure way to deliberately express gratitude. Doing something, however big or small, for another person, the community, or even for Mother Nature (pruning trees, cleaning trash from a river, repotting a plant) is a powerful reminder that we are abundant, because we have enough (time, energy, money) to share—and *all sharing begins with gratitude*.

Putting someone else's needs ahead of yours through an act of service gives that person the nonverbal message that they are valuable and worthy of special time and care. But ultimately when we preform an act of service to someone or something, it helps us to get out of our own way through the unspoken reminder that we aren't here for ourselves, we are here to experience oneness with others and with life itself. This reminder connects us to gratitude so purely that we are then serving the agenda of our Soul.

This is how gratitude prepares us, encourages us, motivates us, and inspires us to *Soulcialize*. It shifts our personal energy and the energy around us. Feeling and expressing gratitude is like gold for relationships in this way. It reminds others that they are seen and appreciated—which is like giving them an "energy hug." Whether it's energetic or physical, this hug releases oxytocin, which is the hormone released through love.

Soulcializing is love made social.

> ### *Your Soul Mission—*
> ### *should you choose to accept it . . .*

* Lift your eyes from this book for a few minutes and take a slow and conscious Visual Visit in your surroundings, feeling into gratitude as you look around the room and experience it in a new way. Make a list in your journal of all that that you see for which you feel genuine gratitude.

* Verbally express your gratitude for three (or more!) people today, looking them in the eyes as you share your appreciation.

Chapter 16

GUIDE #4: INTENTION

Every experience in our life starts with an intention, whether we are making big goals or simply getting out of bed in the morning. All day long, we *unknowingly* produce intentions and achieve their intended results, yet it is by being conscious and deliberate with the process that we make the intentions a conscious and deliberate part of our own life.

An intention is about deciding ahead of time what you want to do and how you want it to turn out, rather than waiting to see what happens and "going from there." It's about deliberate action rather than passive reaction.

You can create an intention for anything; events, relationships, achievements, and even the feelings and energy that you desire *around* those things. By making an emotional and/or energetic intention to connect with others, you are purposely opening your heart, feeling your feelings and expressing them. Actualizing your intentions in this way preps your *Soulcializing* process before it has physically begun.

When you do this on a regular basis, it becomes increasingly apparent to you that you are a larger part of what's being created in your life than you might have ever imagined. The actual setting of an intention is a reminder to consciously direct your thoughts towards your desires and what it takes to achieve them.

Intention versus Wanting

Setting an intention for more connection with others is not the same thing as *wanting* more connection with others. Even if you want something so badly that you find yourself praying for it, it still carries a different energy than creating an intention around it. To "want" something transmits the energy of *request*, whereas to "intend" transmits the energy of *resolve*.

The act of wanting something merely leaves you *feeling the wanting* of that something, whereas setting an intention to bring something forth in your life energetically paves the way for its arrival. This is true because all things in life are manifestations of energy, as we have noted before. An intention is also energy. By setting a specific intention, you draw to you energy that is similar. It's like cutting a swath through a thicket in the jungle. You are creating a pathway by sending your intentions out into the world, and now, that which you wish to create has a direct line back to you.

Clarity

There is a duel dynamic around how intentions should be set that can be confusing. Some teachers tell us to create specific details around our intentions, while others instruct us to release any attachment to specifics around the outcome. The way to get around this apparent contradiction would be to establish distinct details around *how you would like to feel* as a result of your objective being met, versus what you specifically desire that intention to look like, physically.

In this way, you are granting the Universe more leeway for it to respond to your desire and draw it to you. You are releasing your attachment to particulars and are trusting that a wonderful version of what you have intended will manifest in your life.

For instance, with *Soulcializing*, perhaps you have the intention that you would like to be more connected with yourself and others and that you're ready to have the goodness of life flow to you. You can create this result by describing to yourself how it is that you wish to feel as a *result* of this intention being fulfilled.

Imagine to yourself: *I'm going to feel so free, so alive, and open, and allow myself to feel vulnerable.* Then, move into gratitude for this result, *exactly as if it has already occurred.* These two energies put together—intention and gratitude—have been known to produce amazing results.

Choice

When exploring the power of intention it is helpful to keep in mind that intentions may be changed any time you wish. Nothing is set in stone, so you needn't worry that you have set something into motion that you may have no choice about later.

We all make new choices every day. When we're clear about our overall intentions in life, we can make the decisions from a place of ease and confidence, knowing that we can change our mind if we choose to do so.

This is the message of the Soul, from which Soul Courage emerges: Free choice is always yours. This thought alone can support you in the process of creating Intentions without fear.

There are no rules, only opportunities and options. And to overlook any options would be a mistake, for it is the exploration of all of them *before* making a choice that gives you peace of mind, knowing you have considered things carefully and made your best decision.

Behavior Aligning with Intention

There is only one option you may not take: the option to do nothing about what you intend.

All the awesome power of intentions will go nowhere if they are not accompanied by corresponding actions. Simply writing something down on paper, or verbally announcing your desire, doesn't turn it into reality.

For example, if your intention is to be financially abundant, or more connected with your family, then it will behoove you to make sure that the behavior you exhibit is in alignment with that intention. This may seem like a "no-brainer," yet you would be surprised how at many people say one thing and do another.

Yet it's not merely about applying any physical action toward your intention, but also aligning it with the thoughts, feelings, and energy that support that intention. In other words, *all* of you must be involved for your intentions to produce results.

My father shared something invaluable with my sister and me when we were teenagers that I still draw on to this day. I was feeling a bit insecure about a boy in school and wanted some advice. Dad asked me, *"Well, does he like you?"*

I hemmed and hawed a bit and then said, *"Um, he says he does . . . but he hasn't called in almost a week."* (Those were the nights when my sister and I would play endless rounds of rummy beside the phone, waiting for it to ring for at least one of us.)

"*I'd like to tell you both something very important,*" Dad said. "*You never have to* wonder *how someone feels about you or what their intentions are, all you have to do is* watch their feet."

My sister and I looked at each other in confusion and giggled, "*Watch their feet? What does that mean?*"

"*It means,*" he proceeded seriously, "*that someone can talk all they want, but none of it means anything unless they are* moving in the same direction *as what they are saying. Essentially, actions speak louder than words.*"

Whoa. This was a brand-new concept to my 15-year-old brain and it eventually expanded my perspective on topics much larger than wondering about boys. It also taught me a very valuable lesson about myself, and that was:

Who I am is not just who I say I am, nor is it just what I do, nor even what I intend. It is who I am being as a whole.

When you follow your word, beliefs and intentions with actions that are congruent with them, you are demonstrating self-respect and integrity, as well as sending a clear message about your desires to the Universe.

This is what the documentary film *The Secret* was intending to tell us years ago, but it somewhat missed the point, seeming to focus mostly on "wanting" and verbal affirmations, and not enough on the power of combining your energy and actions with what you believe, intend, and desire.

Aligning your behavior with your intention is hugely valuable in holding yourself accountable for everything from relationships to career aspirations to feelings expressed. It's the natural follow up to, and therefore an integral part of, setting an intention, especially so when you are *Soulcializing*.

Ambivalence

Do you remember the childhood game called, "Red light-Green light?" If you recall, everyone would line up side-by-side and all face one person who was a couple hundred yards in front.

The object of the game was to see who could reach the leader in front of everyone first, but the catch was that you could only run towards them when the leader shouted, *"Green light!"* and you would have to freeze on command when they shouted, *"Red light!"*

If you recall, there is no yellow light, therefore The Universe has no choice but to translate any ambivalence into red light energy and freezes on command.

Our objective when setting an intention is to surround it with the feeling of a green light conviction, saying, *"Bring it forth!"* both verbally and nonverbally, physically and energetically.

Unfortunately, your intentions can be unknowingly thwarted by anything from doubt and not believing in the practice, to being embarrassed and feeling foolish, to feeling unworthy of the gift that you are intending to call forth.

When you pour resistance over your intentions, you are projecting opposite energies simultaneously. In other words, you may be feeling and acting in alignment with your intentions, yet emitting fear or uncertainty at the same time.

This mixed message is common and understandable, but meanwhile, back at the ranch, the Universe only responds with results to messages that carry the strong vibration of expansion or contraction—which boils down to two words in the human language: yes and no. It senses all of the confused and indecisive energy, but simply doesn't know what to do with it, and, furthermore, isn't authorized to make the executive decision to cast its outcome. So, since ambivalence energetically shows up as resistance, ambivalent energy eventually shimmies into the "no" category. In essence (*literally*), ambivalence pushes your intentions away.

The energy we attach to our intentions is similar to playing Red light-Green light with the Universe. It's one thing to invite something into your life through your intentions without being confident that you deserve or can produce it, and another thing altogether to send your intentions out with certainty and conviction.

Allowing

We cannot leave this subject of *the energy behind* intentions without touching on one final aspect of that: allowance. Will you *allow* the fruits of all your labor in the garden of your intention to be enjoyed? Believe it or not, some people do not.

For instance, you may have an intention to *Soulcialize* and to bring more wonderful people into your life—maybe even draw to yourself the loving partner for whom you have longed—and you may have overcome any uncertainty, doubt, fear, or ambivalence around that. In fact, you may have everything in place—choice, clarity, conviction, action, *everything*—to produce this intended result, and your desires could still go unmet if you aren't doing your part to *accept the gift*.

This can happen if a person is simply unable to *receive* what has been successfully called forth. It's as if the overnight delivery service leaves a package *that you've ordered* at your front door, and you don't bring it into the house. Or, you bring it into the house, but you won't open it. Or, you open it, but you find something wrong with every part of it. So you send it back.

I have a friend who yearned for years for a lasting romantic relationship. Everyone who knew him also knew that this was his dream. At one point he even told all of his friends that he was "setting his intention" to meet and marry his life partner. So they all started sending ladies his way who they felt would make good "candidates." They made sure he was introduced to all the eligible females they knew. And they watched him really take steps of his own to manifest his goal and end his life's loneliness—they saw that he was earnest in his desire, and not just talking about it. He had begun to take action to back up his intention.

He reached out to more of his contemporaries. He joined groups where he was likely to find a fabulous mixture of interesting and attractive people. He found a book discussion group and also started volunteering at places in need. He really "put himself out there," as they say.

And sure enough, as the months went by several ladies expressed a serious interest in him. But he rebuffed most of them, dated a few of them, and found something wrong with every one of the few to whom he allowed himself to offer some real attention.

His behavior baffled his friends . . . and even baffled himself. But it was not unheard of. Denying final access in this way is very similar to wearing a cloak. The difference is that not allowing the final frontier to be crossed is a passive decline of the flow of energy created by our intentions, whereas a cloak is specifically protecting us as a whole.

Many people have been known to deny themselves exactly what it was they set their intention to experience—the perfect job, the ideal new home, the most wonderful partner, you name it—because once it arrived at their doorstep, they couldn't or wouldn't bring it into their life.

Why?

Because it didn't fit into their story.

Not a small number of human beings have a story about themselves that they don't even know they live. It has become their identity, and they hold onto it for dear life, even if it's *ruining* their life. The story could be titled: *The person to whom nothing good ever happens.* Or: *The man who will always be alone.* Or: *I continue marching on through despair.*

Whatever the scenario, some folks have lived it for so long that it has become their comfort zone and they are afraid to step out of their own pre-written script, because if they do—yes, here we go again—*they don't know how it will end.* So they tough it out, brave it through, and play both the hero and the victim of their story simultaneously.

This confuses the Universe more than ambivalence, because the very thing that you have requested with conviction you reject upon its delivery. A little self-doubt here and there is natural, but after a while consistent non-allowing will begin to reflect to the Universe that you're simply afraid to have what you desire.

If you've seen a theme in this book, this is it: Fear, and the way to overcome it. That's why the book is called Soul Courage. And that's why it has offered a sacred formula, with guides, suggestions, tips, ideas, recommendations, and action steps that can make the formula work in your life.

Soulcializing with Intention

One of the simplest and most promising things that we can do to begin living with the intention to *Soulcialize* is to ask ourselves every morning . . .

How will I love today?

The very question raises our consciousness and gently drops us into our heart, pulling us out of autopilot and aligning us with the reason for our existence. Imagine how our life and the lives of others could open and shift and expand, if we all asked ourselves this one question every day.

Your Soul Mission—
should you choose to accept it . . .

✴ Tomorrow morning before you swing your feet onto the ground, take a moment to consciously breathe in the glory of being awake and alive. Then smile and ask yourself: *How will I love today?*

It's not necessary to have an answer right in the moment, this is more about softly reminding yourself that it's a priority of yours to feel and share love throughout the day. You are declaring that priority through the setting of this intention and you are keeping the reminder to do so fresh, by engaging your mind with a question that it curiously wants to answer. Consider making this a sacred practice every morning and dedicating those morning moments to yourself.

✴ *Inner Gold Star*: Print the question out and tape it to your bathroom mirror, so it's the first thing you see in the morning.

In fact, print a few out and tape them in various places or give them to others!

* Set an intention to connect with others and visually surround those intentions with a green light. Literally feel the forward energy of a green light—maybe even feel yourself surge forward as you did when you were a child, running with gusto when "green light!" was shouted. Take this same energy into your intention for an open heart and deeper connection with life and others. This is saying to your higher self, I'm inviting and allowing myself to receive this, right now.

Chapter 17

GUIDE #5: PRESENCE

Being present is critical for *Soulcializing*. There's simply no way to create a true connection with ourselves, others, and life if we aren't fully present.

Many of us have heard the terms "Mindfulness" and "Awareness." To me they both fit under the heading of a term not so widely used, but more important than those two: Presence.

Mindfulness is a process of the mind, Awareness is a product of the Soul, and Presence is a bridge between the two. Without this bridge the mind and the Soul are operating largely in their own realms. *With* this bridge we have at last found oneness *within*, and can then close the gap between others and ourselves. We can create

Connection—which as we now know is the magic ingredient of *Soulcializing* that allows us to experience the True Self.

We all know the difference between being somewhere physically but not really paying attention, and being fully engaged with our environment or with another person, with no distractions. The second experience is obviously richer than the first, but so often in life we find ourselves consumed with paying attention to what's in our mind rather than what's in our life right now.

If I'm taking a hike because I want to connect with nature, but during the hike I'm pounding through the mountains and my head's filled with a list of things I have to do (*"Okay, pick up dry cleaning, then drop the orders off on the way home, oh, and don't forget to mail those bills today! Yea, okay, and I'll call Dad back while I'm driving."*). Then I'm not being present with nature or myself. I'm not connecting with either one.

When I'm present with nature, my heart is open and I can feel all that's around and inside me (not *think* all that's around and inside me). I notice the breeze and hear the rustle of leaves as the trees sway. I see the squirrels running around and hear the birds singing. (They've been singing all along, but suddenly I hear them, as if someone has just turned on the Hear The Birds switch!) I *feel* the experience around me, and I'm receiving it through my heart in such an enveloping way that it becomes part of me.

This is when a connection is made—when you are so present with someone or something that it feels as if it has become part of you. This is when oneness is experienced.

What is true when I'm present with nature can be true when I am present with myself *wherever* I am. Through what I have called *Soulitude*, I can have this encounter with life any time and any place. It happens when I'm not listening only to the thoughts in my mind, or feeling only the physical movements of my body, but experiencing *all of me* as a whole: body, mind, spirit.

If you connect at such a level, it will feel like *you* are part of *you* again.

Mindfulness

It's important to know that the mind is not your enemy in any of this. It is not opposing you, or somehow "getting in your way." It will be, in fact, your greatest ally as you seek to fulfill the agenda of your Soul—if you use its greatest gift to you, which is mindfulness.

Mindfulness helps us to visualize what we're thinking about in the same way that a film projector displays separate images and pieces them together to make sense. It organizes the things that we know and feel about ourselves, life, and others, categorizing them in a way that allows us to easily determine what is calling for our attention in any given moment—and how we can best and most authentically respond to that.

Mindfulness is like the mind "exercising." It is the mental equivalent of the body working out. Our mind craves mindfulness because it finally gets to do its job *efficiently*, instead of having all of its thoughts just meandering around. It's like following a written list of things to do for the day rather than just wondering or hoping you remember what you need to do.

Mindfulness keeps our mind on track, which eventually increases positive/expanding emotions while reducing negative/contracting emotions. All of this reduces our temptation to fall prey to self-created distractions, and sharpens our focus on exactly what we are being invited to feel and express.

One of the amazing gifts of mindfulness is that it drops all judgment. We simply know and see what is. When we step out of judgment in this way, we step out of neurosis, and when we step out of neurosis we step out of what *we think* we need to be. When we step out of what we think we need to be, our True Selves shine through—which lays the ground for presence.

This is especially helpful when *Soulcializing*, because you are now paying attention to what's happening outside of you *and* inside of you, looking at your exterior experience and your thoughts and feelings without judging, without worrying, and without the tension that those two responses can sometimes produce.

Mindfulness connects how you want to be with how you're now being, integrating the two.

For example, if you have a guest visiting for the weekend, mindfulness invites you not to behave in the same way that you would were others not there. In the morning, you might move about more consciously as you start your day, instead of walking around heavily, preparing your coffee noisily, emptying the dishwasher, or singing in the shower.

If your guest slept in and came down to join you an hour later, you wouldn't speak in a loud voice because you were on your third cup of coffee. You would most likely gently say, *"Good morning,"* and ask how they slept.

Likewise, if *you* were the guest in someone else's home, you wouldn't dream of making a racket in the kitchen before anyone was awake, or making breakfast for yourself and leaving dirty dishes in the sink.

In both instances, you are being mindful of others by being mindful of the energy you carry and create. You are being fully conscious of life and those around you. When we are being fully present in this way, we take ourselves to a uniquely humble place inside, one that can identify with others and see what is best *in* them and *for* them.

But mindfulness is about more than simply being attentive and alert to others, it's also a huge factor in creating our own personal values and monitoring the levels of integrity in us. It offers us a private inner compass around which of our behaviors are acceptable and unacceptable to us (in terms of reflecting our highest thought about who we are), pointing us in the direction that best allows us to align ourselves with that. We then quietly design our life within those parameters, and begin to formulate our personal ideals and standards.

Mindfulness is a state of mind that fills us with compassion and the propensity to reach out to others in ways that reflect kindness and love. This is a wonderful place to live from, and to *Soulcialize* from.

Awareness

While mindfulness can create a wonderful quality of being, its ability to place the fullness of you into any moment in life is limited by the understandings of the mind. Only when those understandings are expanded through the awareness of the Soul can the Whole You be experienced and shared. This is what presence is all about.

Awareness, as I use the term, is a way of looking at life through the eyes and with the perspective of the Soul, which knows not only Who You Are and Why You Are Here, but many other important things as well.

It knows, for instance, that your life is endless; that the conclusion of your present physical expression is not the conclusion of your existence; that life goes on forever. The Soul knows, as well, that there is no separation in the Ultimate Reality. It knows it can't be hurt or damaged in any way. And it knows that love is all there is.

These are things most of us *know* that the Soul knows. What many people have not acquired is the sense of how to apply the Soul's knowing in everyday life. *Soulcializing* is one way to do this.

Awareness is the platform of unity consciousness. Just as the Soul wishes to experience itself through physicality, our body and mind wish to experience themselves as *more* than simply physical. This combined desire of all three parts of our being is what is served by the sacred formula: Feel-Express-Connect, or what I have called Soulitude-Soulrender-Soulcialize.

As our presence with the self and life increases, we feel more aspects of who we truly are. The Soul is constantly merging with our physical being, and the more we pay attention to the fact that this is happening, the thinner the veil between us becomes. When our physical being melds with the Soul, we begin to experience all of the wisdom and clarity that the Soul has deep within.

Awareness is the Soul's natural state. It lives in the peace of an all-knowing consciousness of unity without the distraction of emotions or the orchestration of the mind. It is pure freedom. It needs nothing, and only desires to have a physical expression of itself as a means of experiencing oneness.

The process by which this can often occur for many people is what is presented in the formula offered here. All of the five *Soulcialize* Guides work together, like family escorting you back to yourself. As you start incorporating them into your life, you'll find yourself organically rolling right into the ending point where they produce full presence, and you will have reached the level of *Soulcializing* where you're totally engaging with yourself, others and life at a Soul level.

You will become more separated from separatism and more united with unity, and suddenly feel and know deeply that the Soul is the **Spirit Of** Universal Love. You'll understand that everything is energy and everything that emanates from the collective energy, doesn't *have* a Soul but IS the Spirit of Universal Love.

Presence

We now know that presence is the wonderful quality that emerges when mindfulness and awareness meet. Being present is about watching our thoughts, feelings, and actions, and blending them with the agenda of our Soul throughout the day. This can be monitored by the "Check In" that was described earlier. It allows us to see how the mind can run away from the moment, and how we can return to *right now* by honoring our feelings and expressing them lovingly. It also allows us to observe, with new sensitivity, the needs and behaviors of others, and the larger world around us.

Presence is also about placing our attention on how much and what type of energy we project. How you "show up" in life is a result of the combination of the unique attributes and energy that make you, *you*. The core of you is always the same, but the outer layers—what I want to call your surface energy—can differ from day to day. Even from moment to moment.

It's been said that 90 percent of communication is nonverbal; that our physical energy alone speaks volumes. Body language is a telltale sign of whether you're mostly in your mind or being fully present. If you're with someone physically, but secretly using some of those standard Resistance Techniques we've talked about (your eyes are diverting, you're getting up, shuffling things around, checking your phone, etc.), then you actually aren't truly "with" that other person; you've left that moment.

When you're *Soulcializing*, it's important that you share yourself energetically, emotionally, and physically, showing the other: *"I'm all yours, I'm right here, I see you, I hear you."* I talked about this when I first described how I discovered this third step in the formula that I have found to be so effective in creating Connection in my life.

As I learned in my first "tryout" of this approach with the cashier in the department store, there's no greater display of honor through body language than offering another generous face time. Not only facing them, but maintaining eye contact and allowing them to really see you. Likewise, gifting yourself with really seeing them in return. It's almost as if you are saying to one another, you are important enough to me that I give this moment to you.

The power of eye contact is hugely underrated. The intimacy of eye-to-eye contact is a meeting ground for the Soul, but sadly, there's a lot of discomfort around eye contact in our society *because* it's such an intimate experience. Eye contact isn't about eye gazing or having a lock-down stare, it's about feeling the other person's essence through their eyes. Perhaps you look away naturally, from time to time, but you're not diverting your eyes all over the room while you're facing them. That would simply leave the other person feeling unheard, unseen, and unimportant.

I've created a wonderful way to *Soulcialize* using eye contact that I call "Heart-Eye." It's a simple way to instantly bring about a feeling of more connection with someone when you are in conversation. Most of the time when we're talking with someone and we consciously want to connect with them, we look them right in the eyes. And, sometimes in the sharing of eye contact, we inadvertently have an eye-chasing dance with the other person, trying to connect with them deeper by finding the exact eye that they are using.

Once we start doing this, we notice it happening and begin to think about it while we are supposedly listening to the person. We may even get caught up in some light mind chatter, talking to ourselves about which eye to look at, or wondering if they feel seen and heard. At that point, even though our mind chatter is filled with concern about being present, we are *far* from being present with them because we have moved out of our heart and into our mind.

Something I've found that helps me to stay present and not get drawn into the *eye dance mind chatter* game is to continuously engage in eye contact with the person through their Heart-Eye (the left eye directly over their heart). Not sear into their Heart-Eye like a cyclops, but simply lend presence to them through the eye above the energy of their heart.

Their eyes may dance around for a bit initially, but after a while they subconsciously get the idea that you're staying on the left side and they start returning eye contact to that side of you as well. It sounds almost silly and simple as I write it, but there's something quite magical about this approach; almost as if it were a silent agreement that you are both being more intentional, heart-based, and present.

There is one final element to *Soulcializing* that, while we explored it before, I'd like to bring back into the conversation here as it specifically relates to the idea of presence.

We may be great listeners and seemingly present, yet all the while we may be wearing one of those darn "cloaks!" And as you now know, the quickest, most courageous way to *Soulcialize* is to become aware of any cloaks (invisible layers of protection) that you're wearing, and to consciously discard them.

When we're willing to remove our cloaks and intentionally share our vulnerabilities, we create an instant connection, and we'll feel immense gratitude for it—all of which makes us ever more present.

Ways to shed any existing cloak when seeking to be present include being authentically engaged with the other person in such a way that you are responding to them through your body language without thinking. And without giving a thought to how you are looking or appearing, but just being your natural self. As well, we can choose to be verbally engaged in two-way sharing. Sitting back quietly, saying very little, can be a form of a cloak. So, too, can over-talking and over-sharing. When we practice the art of listening and sharing in a balanced way, we will feel engaged and in-tune with others.

These may seem like simple tools, obvious even to most, but it's amazing how often all of us can forget them when we are not conscious of our behavior . . . when we're not *Soulcializing*. Using the Guides offered here is a way of feeling, expressing, and creating true connection.

Your Soul Mission—
should you choose to accept it . . .

✳ The next time that you're having a conversations with someone (family, friends, or even strangers), be sure that you're gifting them with eye contact and using your Heart Eye as you speak. Then take notice of how different you feel inside.

✳ Think of a time when someone you know was not mindful of a sensitive and caring way to interact with you. Make a note in your Soul Courage Journal of how you felt when encountering their energy. Then, think of a time when you might have been not mindful of someone else's needs. Be honest with yourself about this and make a journal entry about how you might act differently if the same, or nearly the same, set of circumstances should arise again in your life.

Chapter 18

SOUL TEAM

Much has been said in our world about the power of a team. What we've come to realize is that we aren't meant to go it alone, that's why we are all here together.

We know that our lives and the lives of others are greatly enhanced by partnership. Now let's imagine together the possibilities that would open up if we intentionally surrounded ourselves with a group of people who are always cheering us on, and who we find pure joy in cheering on in return. This is a group of Souls with whom we made an agreement before this lifetime, *a Soul contract—if you will*, to support each other and commit to inspiring each other's highest vision about themselves.

A Soul Team.

Most people aren't conscious of their Soul Team, but everyone has one. We all have different levels of awareness around the people who are in our lives, and why they are there. Your Soul Team is that person or group of people with whom you literally feel a sense of being "teamed-up" in life. It could be your parents, your siblings, your best friend, a group of close friends, or even co-workers. You name it. There are no restrictions when it comes to having like-minded Souls in your corner.

We originally get connected with our Soul Team through the energy we carry and emit. We're drawn to each other when the vibrational energetic fields that we emit with our unique energetic signatures are similar. As our vibrations change according to what we focus on, we may attract new people to our team, or other aspects of the people currently on our team.

We can also *consciously* create a Soul Team by intentionally seeking out others with whom we currently resonate. Combining forces is one of the best-kept secrets of happy and successful people.

To build your Soul Team, start by thinking about who you are comfortable around and openly share with them your dreams and struggles, big and small victories, and even the everyday doings of your life. Then offer your support and loving ear to them in return. By doing this, certain people will gravitate toward you, while others may fade away. This will effortlessly create a spiritual and emotional safe place that you will be able to *feel* when you are with your teammates.

When you know who your Soul Team consists of and live *with them* through life, sharing at the level to which I just referred, it fills your heart with ongoing gratitude, and your relationship with each other moves into a place that feels like home— they become family (if they already aren't).

You'll find that you have a natural synergy with them around a multitude of things, and feel close enough to actively collaborate and support one other in being the best you both can be and staying on track in life; spiritually, emotionally, and physically. The mutual gratitude you share with one another will create a consistent and enriching cycle of giving and receiving.

Your Soul Mission—
should you choose to accept it . . .

Close your eyes and think of the people in your life with whom you are closest. Those who you find you gravitate towards and are more comfortable around, the ones who know your joys and pains in life. Without giving it too much thought, jot down the first few names that come to you on a piece of paper (no limit on how many).

Once you have written the list, look it over again, reading each name, and energetically scan your body, from the top of your head, down to your feet, using the energy that you associate with their name. Throughout the process, keep an awareness of how your body reacts to their name and essence.

You will know almost immediately whether there is a safe flow of "yes" as you scan through, or a sign of resistance. After you've done this, cross off any name that may have created tightness in your body when scanning. The names remaining on the list should all be a strong "Yes!" This is your Soul team!

I believe that you have a Soul contract with each of these people. You are both there for and with each other on this journey. You may have even acknowledged this with them already. Remember, this list is not just a team of people that are there for you, but a group of Souls that you should reach out to regularly to check on and acknowledge for their greatness, with assurance that you are there for them, as well.

Chapter 19

PROMISE

Oneness is not just about our individual Souls, but the Souls of the world, which urgently ask us to pass down, with Soul Courage, a model for a new way to be human. This can be the greatest gift we could bequeath the children of our generation, and to theirs.

In a world where technology is expanding at the speed of light, it would befit us to make sure that humanity itself does not fall through the cracks. Children are no longer playing patty-cake and hopscotch in the streets. They're playing video games or listening to iPods, and are equipped with their own phone, expressing themselves through excessive texting and tweeting, or on the walls of Facebook. What they aren't equipped with is the ability to *personally* be with another, and to express themselves verbally, with true feelings of compassion and vulnerability.

The younger generation needs our help. They need *your* help. If you pay close attention, you may notice that children today can't stand still for more than five minutes and don't look you in the eyes when they speak——in fact, they hardly even speak at all. Most of the time they're over-stimulated with two or more handheld or laptop devices running simultaneously. They're losing their "people skills" and, most important, their human nature: Common sense and Soul intuition.

They've become so uncomfortable with the thought of intimacy and simply sharing their feelings that a sense of closeness with another is often created through an insult, badgering, or some sense of negative poking, versus good old-fashioned laughing, being joyful, and speaking from the heart.

It's about time that we asked, *"Why is this new way of living suddenly becoming acceptable to our youth and to us?"; and, "How is it possible that we made such advanced transitioning in our technology, yet handed over the reigns of our Souls at the same time?"*

At the risk of sounding dramatic, I urge you to consider that it is not too late to put a stop to this deeply unconscious and unconnected way of living.

It's alarming to think that the younger generation will become adults one day and run the world, passing down its distorted value system. Even the adults who were born in a slower and easier time are also getting caught up in the fast-paced energy that's being saturated in the world. And they are usually unconscious of it all, unless or until they experience an earth-shattering change that "wakes" them up.

But this is where the rubber meets the road, the turning point, where truth promotes change: We needn't go through extreme lows in our life in order to feel the true essence of the Soul. In fact, it may be the exploring of the very questions with which we started this book—*Who are You?* and *Why are you here?*—that create the opportunity to by-pass those "lows," unveiling a new perspective on the reasons for physical life.

This place of questioning creates the fertile ground we've been seeking for a new way of living, one that we can enthusiastically hand over to the younger generation. With the sociology of our current understanding being a study of human beings and their culture, the resulting behavior is one that our society approves of and expects. But a new approach to human behavior, which I call *Soulciology*, could produce a celebration of Souls and an exploration into their connectedness, encompassing behavior that our society does *not* expect, but loves when it encounters it.

The movement toward this new *Soulciological* behavior is within our reach. It can readily become a way of living collectively when we start by embracing it individually . . . all which happens automatically when we *Soulcialize* and hold the thought that there are no new connections, only Souls reconnecting through a promise made to one another (pre-physical life) that we will never let each other forget who we are.

Let's keep that promise.

> *Your Soul Mission—*
> *should you choose to accept it . . .*

* Realign the hearts of at least two children today by bringing them back into the present moment. Whether it's through a hug, a joke that makes their heart open, or just looking in their eyes and smiling, showing them that they are seen. Bring them back by reminding them of who they are in their Soul.

Chapter 20

MOMENT

It is said that a "realization" is the state of being realized. And I believe that when we, as humans, move to a deep and significant realization of the Soul, we are coming full circle by experiencing our True Selves. And so we end here where we began: We are Souls, having come here with an agenda. Our agenda is to experience the truth of our oneness with all of life.

When we understand this, we begin to see that it is our Soul that can motivate the decisions we make in our life if we allow it to.

When we begin to see that our Soul can motivate our decisions, we begin to trust life more, *and unconditionally.*

When we trust unconditionally, we allow ourselves to feel more.

When we feel more, we begin to have the courage to express ourselves from the most real and authentic place.

When we express ourselves from the most real and authentic place, we become more comfortable in our skin and don't live from fear.

When we no longer live from fear, we become invulnerable.

When are become invulnerable, we are free.

When we are free, we give others the courage to set themselves free, and then they turn around and do the same for another.

And the circle continues . . . because we have lived with Soul Courage.

There comes a time in all of our lives when we take a look at ourselves and say: *This is no longer who I am.*

It's as if, in that moment, we suddenly catch on, click in, and are transported to a place of deep and sudden knowing that unveils in us a new perspective on the reasons for physical life.

We feel no shame, only an awareness that *it is time* to shift out of the old, protective, and non-serving ways, and move back home to our True Self.

This point, this moment, this spark of awareness . . . this is your body and mind aligning with your Soul. It is your moment of Soul Courage.

Ahhhh . . . congratulations, you have arrived.

Now, watch what happens.

AFTERWORD

Thank you for courageously being open to the ideas in this book. I truly believe that everything we desire to know is already inside of us, held gently in our Soul. There is no author greater than you, for your life. My wish for you is that you live through the magnificence of your Soul Courage, as I trust that it will put you in touch with this truth, opening your heart and the hearts of all those with whom you connect.

Please be compassionate with yourself as you try the suggestions in this book, and allow yourself to move into full feeling and expression at whatever rhythm and pace with which you resonate. This is what will create your own unique doorway to the freedom of Soul Courage.

My hope is that you close the cover of this book knowing that many Soul friends await you, starting with me. If the thought of expanding your Soul Team brings you joy, please stay in touch.

There are resources in place to support you on your Soul Courage journey and keep you connected in a gathering of like-minded Souls.

You're invited to join the interactive community at *www.soulcourage.com*, where you may share your thoughts and engage with others in the online blog. You will also find a *Soul Courage Online Course*, and a wonderful collection of heartfelt *Soulebrate* greeting cards, specifically designed to increase the connectedness among us all.

And please join me on Facebook at the Soul Courage Community to continue our connection and become part of the Soul Courage domino effect, where we lead by example and pass the torch on to others.

Love, from my Soul to yours—

XO,
Tara-jenelle

ABOUT THE AUTHOR

TARA-JENELLE WALSCH is the founder and spirit behind the *Soulebrate* greeting card company and the *Soulcialize* personal development program. *Soulebrate* greeting cards are sold worldwide, carrying her original designs and personal messages of encouragement and empowerment. Tara-jenelle speaks publicly about building emotional awareness and greatly enhanced living through the *Soulcialize* concept, which she believes create soul connection and has the ability to enrich the world at large.

"Your only obligation in any lifetime is to be true to yourself."
—Richard Bach

Related Titles

If you enjoyed Soul Courage, you may also enjoy other Rainbow Ridge titles. Read more about them at *www.rainbowridgebooks.com*.

God's Message to the World: You've Got Me All Wrong
by Neale Donald Walsch

*Coming Full Circle: Ancient
Teachings for a Modern World*
by Lynn Andrews

*Consciousness: Bridging the Gap Between
Conventional Science and the New
Super Science of Quantum Mechanics*
by Eva Herr

Jesusgate: A History of Concealment Unraveled
by Ernie Bringas

Messiah's Handbook: Reminders for the Advanced Soul
by Richard Bach

Blue Sky, White Clouds
by Eliezer Sobel

Inner Vegas: Creating Miracles, Abundance, and Health
by Joe Gallenberger

When the Horses Whisper
by Rosalyn Berne

Channeling Harrison, Book 1
by David Young

Lessons in Courage
by Bonnie Glass-Coffin and don Oscar Miro-Quesada

Dying to Know You: Proof of
God in the Near-Death Experience
by P.M.H. Atwater

The Cosmic Internet: Explanations from the Other Side
by Frank DeMarco

Afterlife Conversations with Hemingway:
A Dialogue on His Life, His Work and the Myth
by Frank DeMarco

Dance of the Electric Hummingbird
by Patricia Walker

Rainbow Ridge Books publishes spiritual, metaphysical, and self-help titles, and is distributed by Square One Publishers in Garden City Park, New York.

To contact authors and editors, peruse our titles, and see submission guidelines, please visit our website at *www.rainbowridgebooks.com*.